M000083188

# PRAISE FOR SHASHEEN SHAH AND
# THE KID AND THE KING

"*The Kid and the King* will take you on an epic journey into your soul and will help you come out feeling like you can conquer the world! Read it. Live it. Love it!"

—*JOHN ASSARAF,*
New York Times *Best-selling Author & CEO of MyNeurogym.com*

"Shasheen brings a heartfelt and refreshingly insightful look at the question of how and why we communicate and act the way we do with a field-tested set of exercises and questions that are bound to make a difference in how you look at yourself and your team."

—*CLAUDE SILVER,*
*Chief Heart Officer of VaynerMedia*

"*The Kid and the King* wastes no time tapping directly into how what's fueled our lives to reach insane levels of success could be the same fuel that burns it all down if we don't get conscious of what it is, how it works, and what to do about it. Taking the time to walk through the 5 steps, and then continuing to apply them, will help us ultimately reign in our insatiable desire for achievement and help us connect instead with the art of fulfillment and peace."

—*MARI TAUTIMES,*
*former CEO, Western Asset Protection and author of #keepgoing:*
From 15-Year-Old Mom to Successful Entrepreneur and CEO

"When I met Shasheen several years ago, on the surface, it appeared as if I were as a high a performer as they come. I had great career success and trajectory. Plus, I was physically fit, constantly worked on self-development, ate only natural foods, had a beautiful family, went on fun vacations and adventures, and lived in a great place in California. But the real story is I was beyond run down, brain fogged, and on the verge of the scene from *Anchorman*—picture Will Ferrell's character saying, 'I'm in a glass cage of emotion.'

"My work with Shasheen and the EMP Process has not only continued to grow all the areas of life people would consider 'success,' but most important of all is that I have a dramatically improved life experience, more presence, better relationships, and hands down, I am happier every single day. I started living life more the way I truly wanted, with clearer priorities and not just to continue to do 'what you are supposed to' or makes other people happy. The return on the investment for the work we have done is invaluable.

"And the best part of what I learned is that nothing is broken, I do not need to be fixed, and I am simply human like everyone else. Once I grasped that, my ability to connect and coach others (at work and in personal relationships) has taken off, and I believe I am making a profound impact as a leader more than ever. By embracing that humanity, seeking to understand it, and finding out what triggers me and what drives my emotions, I am able to see the game more clearly. The triggers never stop, but the ability to navigate life, stress, and incredible challenges just becomes easier."

—*CHRIS SULLIVAN,*
*Senior Manager at Tesla*

*"A Paint by Number Process to Create the Masterypiece of Your Life!"*

"Finally, a process anyone can learn. Your paintbrush will be your willingness to follow the 5 magical steps of the Emotional Mastery Process or (EMP). When you mix the colors of your inner critic, with your inner essence and introduce them to your inner coach, the result is a brand-new color called harmony. Using the EMP as your palette, you will paint the life you've always dreamed was possible. As you teach your inner critic to shake hands with your inner coach, they will create a life-long partnership of fulfillment, prosperity, purpose, and joy!

"When The Kid finally, reluctantly, releases his grip on the paintbrush, instead of yanking it out of his hand, The King will thank him as he gently takes control of the brush, rinses it clean, and then begins to paint the masterypiece that will become the prized possession of the gallery. "A life well lived; worth living."

—BOBBY KOUNTZ,
*Author, Speaker, Sobriety Scholar, Inspirationalist*

"Shasheen's coaching gets straight to the point. His insights cut swiftly through your self-imposed, limiting beliefs. Opening yourself or your team to that perspective will begin your own transformation toward outcomes at rates and scopes you'd previously only dreamed about."

—BERNIE MALONEY,
*Systems Operation Manager, Hewlett Packard*

"Having Shasheen in your corner sets you up for success and promotes thinking from different angles to see past the obvious. His fresh ideas, resourcefulness, and talent resulted in outstanding achievements on my part, and I couldn't recommend this gentleman more."

—OLIVER HARTWIG,
*Pura Vida Villas, Phuket, Thailand*

"Shasheen has been an incredible, life-changing asset to me. . . . I'm a completely different thinker today. I have that peace I've been striving for, and I thank Shasheen for getting me there in short order."

—SHARON CONTILLO,
*Board Member, Women in Film & Video US*

# THE
# KID
## AND THE
# KING

The Hidden Inner Struggle High Achievers Must
Conquer to Reignite and Reengage with Life

SHASHEEN SHAH

**Disclaimer:** The content of this book is based on the author's professional and personal experience and research. This book is not a substitute for professional health advice, diagnosis, or treatment. Always seek the advice of a qualified health provider with any questions you have regarding mental health or the appropriateness of any therapy mentioned or any activity herein.

*Published by*

**Coherent Strategies LLC**

TELLURIDE, CO

Copyright © 2021 Shasheen Shah

ISBN-13: 978-0-578-94472-2

Edited by Carol Killman Rosenberg

Interior by Gary A. Rosenberg

# Contents

*To you, the reader, for the curiosity that
has brought you to this place in your journey.
May the concepts and ideas put forth in the following
chapters light up a path that brings you more love,
compassion, joy, gratitude, and adventure!*

# Introduction

There is nothing wrong with you . . .

There is nothing to fix; nothing is broken.

Yet, you experience an inner struggle.

Why?

Since the beginning, men and women have found themselves battling against not only external enemies but also struggling with something hidden inside themselves. You've experienced this. You've had that sense that, despite whatever accomplishments you have achieved, your life still isn't what you want it to be. You have dreams—and then you experience fear. You have a vision—and then you tell yourself you are too old, too young, too tired, too fat, too busy, too *something* to do it. You procrastinate.

Yes, you've achieved impressive goals and outcomes in life, but now you can't seem to find the drive you need to climb the next mountain. You know how to climb mountains, but you don't understand why the tools you've used to reach the summit are failing to deliver results now. This inner struggle may have left you feeling exhausted and confused.

The enemy in this struggle has gone by many names: the inner demon, resistance, shadow self, gremlin, and others. The self-help industry has put forward two solutions to this struggle: The first is all-out warfare: discipline, dominance, destruction, and more structure—whatever it takes to defeat the demon and achieve success. This warfare approach has a few predictable outcomes. Inarguable results of this enemy strategy are one. This method has been recommended for millennia because it can produce results and bring success in the targeted area. Sadly, the trade-offs achievers have made to create this success have left them (and perhaps you) feeling depleted, unsure, alone, and misunderstood. Many people find the success they fought so hard to achieve has exacted a high price: rocky relationships, ill health, and a vague sense of purpose.

Another common side effect of the warfare approach is a loss of motivation. Life becomes suboptimal. Perhaps you've felt your fire going out. You just don't have the motivation and engagement for your work or life that you had when you were younger. You've run out of inner fuel. Achievers who are too tired to climb another hill tend to just accept "lives of quiet desperation," to quote Thoreau. And some, as I did, turn to other harmful distractions to numb the disquiet inside. Ultimately, all this struggle and confusion and not living up to one's expectations is quickly followed by other results: frustration, shame, and guilt.

The second approach to this struggle is the exact opposite of warfare. It's just to observe the inner demon nonjudgmentally and without emotion. This awareness method can certainly end the constant and never-ending struggle. But it often comes with a side of awareness hell, because merely observing the demon without taking action fails to make it behave. At its worst, this path can lead someone to a life that never comes close to reaching their potential. Of course, this brings us back to frustration, shame, and guilt.

Here are the questions so many achievers and leaders ask me and you may be wondering yourself:

+ "How do I live a life of achievement *and* peace."

+ "How do I fulfill the potential I know I have *without* the exhausting daily warfare with myself?"

+ "I'm smart and accomplished. Why do I do some stupid things?"

## THE WAY OF THE KID AND THE KING

*If you are a woman, replace the word* **King** *with* **Queen** *throughout the book;* **King** *is used for simplicity's sake, but the work described here can help both high-achieving men and women reignite and reengage with life.*

Since you're reading this book, it is safe to assume that the other two paths have let you down in some way; those methods just haven't worked for you or have stopped working for you. So, here I share a third way, which has transformed the lives of my high-achieving clients, as well as my own. It's the way of the Kid and the King, and it can change your life.

Allow me first to share an important principle: Transformations in art, business, and science, as well as in life in general, can come from something as simple as a relationship or perspective shift. Consider this:

+ As a martial artist progresses toward mastery, she learns to look at an opponent's attacks not as a hostile force but as a force that can help her defeat a bigger, stronger opponent. She has transformed her relationship with a hostile force into one of an ally. Increased power and effectiveness result.

+ Systems thinking has transformed businesses the world over. Leaders learned to stop thinking of their company as a collection of departments and functions and started seeing it as a cohesive, interdependent system. This new relationship with their businesses revealed new paths to products, productivity, and profits.

+ Doctors once believed that peptic ulcers were caused by anxiety and stress. Then Drs. Barry Marshall and Robin Warren discovered that the bacteria *H. pylori* was the culprit by looking at the problem from a new perspective. The discovery turned decades of medical doctrine upside down, earned Marshall and Warren a Nobel Prize in 2005, and ended the suffering of millions.

You see, a simple shift in understanding can transform your life and world. I experienced one of these transformational shifts twenty years ago after watching a movie, of all things: Ron Howard's Academy Award–winning film *A Beautiful Mind*.

This movie is about an extraordinary, real-life mathematician, John Forbes Nash Jr., who was being driven by three distinct aspects of his personality, which appeared to him as "real" people but separate from himself. These identities caused him to act in ways that seemed irrational to outside observers. Nash ultimately triumphed over the debilitating effects of his schizophrenia. He did it not by getting rid of the voices in his head but by changing his adversarial relationship to them. He called this a "diet of the mind." As a result, Nash was able to navigate the rest of his life and was recognized for his life's work when he won the Nobel Prize for Economics in 1994.

At the end of the movie, I realized that, metaphorically, I had a similar relationship with the voices in my head—the demon, resistance, gremlin, or whatever you call it. I knew myself to be bright and capable, but some of the things I'd say to myself and the behaviors I took on as an adult made no sense to me or, often, to others around me. I was *not* on a diet of the mind. Instead, I was on a diet of self-medication and other distractions and addictions to deal with my confusion.

So rather than continue to struggle and fight against my demon, I decided to make peace with him by changing my relationship to him. First, I changed how I talked about this part of me (the language we use is incredibly powerful). No longer was it a demon or a gremlin or resistance; it was merely . . . the Kid.

I no longer sought to defeat or silence the Kid. Instead, I made peace with him. So, there was nothing for me to fix or get rid of or fight. I also realized that this part of me would be with me for the rest of my life, so it made more sense to create a new relationship with him than to spend the rest of my life struggling against him.

When I made this relationship shift, I learned to see the Kid for some of the good he was trying to do. Just like the martial artist discovers to use an opposing force to achieve success, I learned to appreciate and use what the Kid offered me. Most important, I learned how to get the Kid to let go of the steering wheel and take a seat in the back while the King (my adult self) drove my life forward.

When I stopped struggling, I had more energy. (It's incredible how much of our daily energy is used up in this continuous struggle against the Kid.) And, as I gained more energy, I was also gifted with more clarity. Free of the struggle, both parts of me were now able to see and think and dream again. I found myself reignited and reengaged with life. This perspective shift was life changing.

Since then, I've had the privilege of working with remarkable men and women in my coaching practice, including world leaders, CEOs, high achievers in Fortune 500 companies, and maverick entrepreneurs who have created multimillion-dollar successes. When my clients began to change their relationship with the Kid, they also began experiencing life-transforming changes. For example:

- There was the high-achieving, multimillion-dollar financier who was unfulfilled and unengaged with his work and his relationships with his wife and kids. When he learned to put the King in the driver's seat, he left his job and created two new businesses that gave him time with his family.

- There's the national political leader who realized his Kid was driving the bus, and he was approaching all his opponents with the same fight and struggle. When he saw how to change the relationship with his Kid, he also learned to change his approach and relationships with both political allies and enemies. He went on to achieve victory and gain new levels of national leadership.

- There was the accomplished female executive who found herself, bewilderingly, in dysfunctional relationships—both with men and her business. As she came to understand her Kid, she set herself free to become president of a new company she enjoyed more and is now in a healthy relationship and engaged to be married.

I want you to experience the breakthroughs and transformations that my clients and I have experienced. I want you to be reignited and reengaged with your life and in your relationships. Simply put, I want you to gain a better experience of life. This process is a journey to emotional mastery, and you will see it referred to in this book as the Emotional Mastery Process (EMP). It begins with understanding your Kid, changing your adversarial relationship with that part of you, and then putting your King in charge.

Here's the journey I take my clients on and the one you will be following throughout this book:

- **Chapter 1:** In an eye-opening, three-minute exercise, you'll see, perhaps for the first time, just how much this inner struggle has impacted your life and energy.

+ **Chapter 2:** You'll learn how the Kid has fueled your past achievements and understand why that fuel has flamed out. You'll also discover what the King uses for fuel and how it can take you to the next level.

+ **Chapter 3:** You'll discover just how much your responses and reactions to life events are driven by the Kid—and how to start putting the King in charge.

+ **Chapter 4:** With a better understanding of the Kid and the King, you'll learn a few important philosophical principles that impact how you react, motivate you, and create your future.

+ **Chapter 5:** I'll explain a simple practice to help you integrate the principles of the Kid and the King into your daily life experience, using the 5 EMP Questions to guide your mind.

+ **Chapter 6:** You'll discover how EMP can bring you deep insights into your life from everyday events.

+ **Chapter 7:** You'll understand how simple misperceptions can rob you of joy and fulfilment, as well as how to regain control of those perceptions in a way that leads you to a better life.

+ **Chapter 8:** You'll gain the insight you need to experience more joy and satisfaction in life and eliminate much of the inner struggle you are facing.

+ **Chapter 9:** You'll explore the source from which your emotions arise. And perhaps, most important, you'll learn what *not* to do when you experience strong emotions.

+ **Chapter 10:** Ultimately, the course of your life is determined by the actions you take and don't take. As you'll learn, emotional mastery comes from moving from *reaction* to *action*.

+ **Chapter 11:** The future and outcomes you desire determine the actions you take today. By answering questions like "Whose outcome am I really pursuing?" and "Am I even pursuing an outcome?" you'll develop a different perspective on your future.

+ **Chapter 12:** Watch your language! You'll learn some new tools and directions that can accelerate you on your journey to emotional mastery.

+ **Chapter 13:** Sometimes the most powerful way to move ahead is to be still. I'll share a powerful five-minute stillness practice that will speed your journey on the path to emotional mastery.

+ **Chapter 14:** Both your past and future impact where you are on your journey. As you'll learn, one of the greatest shortcuts to emotional mastery is pausing to examine the early sources of your core identity.

+ **Chapter 15:** When you ask yourself some hard questions and face the answers with courage, you'll be rewarded with a remarkable leap forward into freedom and joy.

+ **Chapter 16:** Regardless of success, wealth, position, or power, everyone has an edge to their comfort zone. You'll discover how to journey past your edge so that you can continue to grow rather than fall short of your potential.

+ **Chapter 17:** Masters of a craft use tools to create their masterpieces. You'll gain all the tools you need to paint your own masterpieces, the desired outcomes of your life.

Your journey to a reengaged, reignited life begins in the next chapter. Turn the page, and you will understand your inner struggle in a way you never have before.

# CHAPTER 1

# Seeing What You've Always Known for the First Time

"You're kidding, right?"

"No," I say.

"Seriously?"

"I'm serious—how long has that been there? I love the architecture."

"How many years have you lived here?" she asks.

"Thirteen," I say.

"Then you've been driving by that building almost every day for thirteen years. They built this back in the early seventies!"

I was silent for a while. How was it possible that I had driven past a highly visible building with unique architecture for more than a dozen years? Here's what was different: I needed a lift to the airport, and I was in the passenger's seat. Every time I had driven by the building, I was focused on the sharp turn just ahead to the left, so my head was always facing the opposite direction.

During our first session together, when I take my clients through the exercise in this chapter, they have the same reaction I did when I realized I'd been driving past the building without seeing it for so many years: "How could I not have seen that before?"

The realization is profound, and it's the doorway to forever changing your relationship with this inner struggle. Are you ready to walk through the door to the rest of your life? You are going to see something about your personality and identity that you've never noticed before. You will clearly see the inner struggle that's been with you for your entire life.

## EXERCISE: *Your 5-5 Personality Inventory*

My journey into the question of my identity started at a young age. One of my first therapists asked me to write down what I like about myself and what I want to change. This gave me important insight and laid the foundation for this 5-5 personality inventory. This exercise has three simple steps. Don't read step 3 until you have completed steps 1 and 2. What you discover may shock you, as it did me.

### STEP 1: *What do you like about yourself?*
### *Who are you at your best?*

What are you most proud of about yourself? What would make you feel the most pride to have someone say about you? These are ways of being and showing up in the world rather than specific skill sets. For example, "I am hardworking, intelligent, generous, collaborative, and trustworthy." Okay, it's your turn. Write your list:

_____

_____

_____

_____

_____

_____

_____

**STEP 2:** *What don't you like about yourself? What aspects of your personality would you like to change?*

These are negative traits that you might say typically get in the way of getting what you want. For example, "I am judgmental, critical, impatient, selfish, and careless." Believe it or not, this is sadly often easier for people to complete than the positive aspects. Write your list:

_____

_____

_____

_____

_____

_____

Before you read ahead, take a moment to make your list.

When I first did my personality inventory, I was surprised by what I discovered. Here are my responses, so that you can judge for yourself:

*I am gregarious, compassionate, and aware of others' needs.*
*I am intelligent, strategic, and loving.*
*I am also a procrastinator, overly critical, judgmental, intolerant, and a rebel.*

As I read through my lists, what hit me for the first time was the opposition, the struggle, the duality between these two aspects of myself. Right before me was an inner struggle that had caused much trouble in my life. It became even more apparent when I blended the two lists together. How could it be that I was

> *A gregarious, intolerant rebel? An intelligent, critical procrastinator? A compassionate, judgmental critic? A loving, intolerant man aware of others' needs? There was a war within me between two opposing forces.*

### Step 3: *Merge Your Lists*

Take a moment to merge your two lists together like I did in the above example. Start by finding the most polar opposite attributes and blending them together into a paragraph. This will instantly give you a better sense of this internal war within. Write your paragraph here:

_____

_____

_____

_____

_____

_____

_____

## PERSONAL INVENTORY CLIENT EXAMPLES

I've discovered that the same war that was raging inside me also rages inside my clients. No matter how successful, they all had this inner struggle wreaking havoc on their life experience. This inner struggle has been going on at the periphery of their consciousness. Unnoticed, it was sapping away their energy and engagement and enjoyment of life. There, in the shadows, it was making them feel like something just isn't right despite having achieved success by anyone's standards.

Let me introduce you to three clients I've had the privilege to lead through the Emotional Mastery Process to a reengaged, reignited life. I believe their stories and struggles will help you better understand your own. You'll begin to see how much you have in common with other high achievers and, at the same time, how unique your personal struggle is.

### Meet Simon

Simon is a maverick entrepreneur. He came from a broken home. When he grew up and moved out into the world, he was exposed to people who threw their degrees around. They were playing a rigged game he couldn't join because he didn't have the grades or the family money to back him. He was not part of the system, and that world was closed to him. So, he went on to show them. He earned millions of dollars and grew a successful business. Yet, for all those millions, he felt unsettled, misunderstood, and alone. He didn't feel like the success everyone else saw him as.

Here is how Simon described what he liked about himself: *hardworking, determined, focused. honorable, and a good boss.*

Simon also described himself as *impatient, impulsive, frustrated, self-critical,* and *judgmental.*

When those were merged together, here's how Simon's inner struggle manifested:

*I am a good boss who is hardworking, determined, and focused, and who can become frustrated easily and be impulsive. I'm also an honorable man who is focused and yet impatient and very judgmental of others.*

Clearly, Simon was at war with himself.

## Meet David

David excelled in school—straight As, high SAT scores, and strong athletics. His unmatched drive to succeed took him to the top of his class at Harvard, and it landed him a dream job in investment banking. He crushed whatever challenge his parents or school or business put in front of him. He was rewarded with praise and promotions from his superiors and a lifestyle envied by others.

But life had lost its color for him. He couldn't put his finger on it, but he was losing his motivation and drive. His fuel ran dry. His relationships with his wife and children also began to weaken. And when he was promoted into an upper-management leadership role in his company, he experienced something for the first time in his life—failure. All his high-performer skills weren't translating into leadership success. Why couldn't his team perform as well as he had? David is not alone in this struggle; in the larger corporations I consult with, this theme comes up often. Leadership requires more than personal performance.

Here is how David described what he liked about himself and what he wanted to change:

David described himself as *"smart, disciplined, strong at presentations and public speaking, a hard worker, self-aware, and sensitive."*

David also described himself as *"arrogant, self-centered, impatient, and critical of others."*

Here is how David's inner struggle manifested:

> *I am a smart and disciplined, sensitive, and arrogant, self-aware guy who has a strong work ethic and presentation skills and who gets very critical and impatient with others.*

## Meet Susan

Susan was the president of a large company. She was capable, smart, and drove performance. Whatever she turned her hand to, she excelled at. Her employees admired her leadership style. Tough but fair, she was excellent at bringing out the best ideas and performance in others. She was charming, respected, and all business at the same time. She created winning teams. She had total respect and confidence from the board of directors as she outperformed herself quarter after quarter.

Yet, as good as Susan was at creating a winning team at work, she couldn't seem to create a winning team at home. After a failed marriage, she had several short-term relationships but couldn't make anything last. She was successful but struggled with loneliness.

Susan described herself as *"hardworking, a good leader, empathetic, principled, and strategic."*

She also described herself as *"self-critical, a procrastinator, compulsive, and negative."*

And here's how Susan's inner struggle manifested:

> *I am a strategic, hardworking, and empathetic leader who is very negative, compulsive, and impatient and who tends to procrastinate. I am both self-critical and principled.*

As you can see, you are not alone in your inner struggle. And, at the same time, your internal conflict is as unique to you as your thumbprint. So, how do we deal with this struggle?

As I said in the introduction, there are three options. One is an all-out war. The other is passive observation, and the third path, the way of the Kid and the King, is making peace with and creating an entirely new relationship with the Kid. But you won't be able to achieve this without first understanding why the Kid has so much control over your life.

*If you want to live successfully in this world, you will have to embrace the duality within yourself and come to a reconciliation with who you are and what you truly want. Otherwise, your unreconciled selves (your Kid and your King) will continually leave you feeling like there's more, like you're never fully complete . . . like an imposter.*

In the next chapter, we will look at how the Kid has come to dominate your very core motivation—your fuel. You'll discover why that Kid fuel eventually runs out. And you'll learn how to tap into the King's fuel that can take you to the next level of performance and a reignited life. This reignited life comes not through an inner war and not through passive observation but through a new relationship within oneself that brings peace and freedom.

# CHAPTER 2

# Your Fuel System

You've seen this a thousand times; it's in every action-adventure movie you've ever seen: There's the hero, beaten, down-and-out, face in the dirt. Failure is certain. He has no strength or will to fight on. Then he discovers a new motivation. Perhaps someone's life is in jeopardy or he hears or remembers a message of hope. With this new source of motivation, this new fuel, the hero rises from the ashes to defeat the enemy and achieve victory. This same story-telling device has been used for thousands of years. Why? Because it reveals a truth that all of us know at a deep level—our fuel runs out. It has an expiration date. The only way to reach the next level of performance, achievement, and success is to find a new fuel source.

One of the most common struggles my high-achieving clients come to me with is that their motivation has dried up and they can't understand why. They may describe the feeling, like "I've just lost my drive," or "I'm just going through the motions." Often, they say, "I just don't have any passion for anything anymore. What's wrong with me?" What's going on here?

In this chapter, you'll discover that much of your achievement and success has been driven by Kid fuel, which eventually runs out. And once it does, the answer is to tap into King fuel, which will take you higher and further with less force. But to understand what's going on, we have to go back—way back.

## SEEKING LOVE AND APPROVAL

Once upon a time, you were a baby. When you first made your appearance, your life was filled with an endless amount of *oohing* and *ahhing*, praise, adoration, and affection from the adults around you. Your every need was attended to instantly. Every small achievement you made was rewarded with love and approval.

Your first sounds—approval and affection

Your first smile—praise and hugs

Your first wave—a celebration and all sorts of people returning your gesture

Your first steps—squeals of delight!

You received endless unconditional love and approval simply for existing and doing what babies do. But then you began toddling out a bit more. You began to assert your independence. Suddenly, your world became a little more restricted. There was "No!" Suddenly, gates and locks kept your curious mind and little hands out of places you wanted to venture.

There are consequences. You are expected to be a good boy or good girl. You begin to earn your good stamp of approval and love by your actions. You quickly become conditioned to follow the guidelines—both the spoken and unspoken rules of the tribe. Simply put, love and approval aren't unconditional anymore. You have to perform to earn your "emotional cookie." Psychologist Erik Erikson astutely describes this struggle through the first three stages of childhood development: 1) Trust vs. Mistrust, 2) Autonomy vs. Shame and

Doubt, and 3) Initiative vs. Guilt. By the time you're five years old, not only is the need to be loved well established, but it's also safe to say that trust, shame, and guilt issues abound.

In some cases, the way to earn love and worth isn't by pleasing but by proving. Instead of gaining approval by pleasing others, provers seek it by proving their worth by winning the outward symbols of success others admire: power, position, money, possessions, and so on. The great irony is that provers are still seeking love and approval by ultimately attaining what others see as worthy. The prover's Kid is seeking approval and attention just as much as the pleaser's Kid is seeking approval and attention.

This quest for other people's love and approval is the beginning of your hidden inner struggle between the Kid and the King. Few realize how pervasive this early conditioning affects us in adult life. One of my earliest influences, Jiddu Krishnamurti, describes it best in his book *Freedom from the Known*:

> How can we be free to look and learn when our minds from the moment we are born to the moment we die (...) have been conditioned by nationality, caste, class, tradition, religion, language, education, literature, art, custom, convention, propaganda of all kinds, economic pressure, the food we eat, the climate we live in, our family, our friends, our experiences—every influence you can think of—and therefore our responses to every problem are conditioned. Are you aware that you are conditioned?

Now, as you worked to navigate this reality successfully, the Kid was in charge of driving the bus. How else could it be? The adult you, your King, wasn't on the scene yet. And the fuel your Kid uses to drive the bus is other people's love and approval. It is an insatiable need to be seen. In transactional analysis (TA), this insatiable need is referred to as strokes.

For many of us, this motivational fuel of love and approval-seeking is what powers most of our achievements and accomplishments into middle adulthood. Your Kid has been driving the bus on high-octane love and approval- and attention-seeking. And then the fuel runs out. Here's why: Trying to motivate yourself by seeking love and approval and acceptance of others predictably loses its motivation the older you get. The provers say, "I'm going to conquer or achieve this no matter what! I'll show them!" The good boy or girl will step up and dutifully stay on the path, regardless of the cost. Burnout and confusion are inevitable. When my clients finally get to me, they are too tired to continue doing what they've always done and aren't sure how to move forward.

## THE KID'S WAY

The Kid has also been influencing your strengths and weaknesses. In the previous chapter, you looked at what you do and do not like about yourself. Most people quickly see how many of the traits they don't like are Kid conditioning—or Kid logic, as I call it. In 1961, psychiatrist Eric Berne observed that kids develop a plan for their life as a strategy for physical and psychological survival and will often stick with that strategy the rest of their life.

Your Kid wanted to earn love and approval and attention. So, your Kid reached for the closest strategy at hand that would accomplish this. If it worked, it became the go-to strategy the Kid used to achieve love and worth. There is nothing wrong with being gifted and having strengths. You owe most of your success to them. But these Kid-conditioned gifts can be problematic:

First, that strategy doesn't work in every circumstance. Let me use myself as an example: My Kid found that being gregarious was a great way to get love, attention, and approval from others. It helped me navigate my family, make friends, and get me jobs. My Kid loved that strategy! But as I moved further into adulthood and into leadership roles, suddenly that gregariousness approach stopped working and was no longer a valid approach. There were times and places that it cost me dearly. Just two examples of how this blunted my leadership and personal life are poor boundaries with subordinates and avoiding difficult but necessary conversations.

In truth, I had many more gifts waiting to be explored and mastered by my King. But my Kid couldn't see them. He was like a guy who goes into the gym and only does bicep curls with one arm and then leaves. That's an incredible bicep! But also a severely deformed physique!

My dad was a man of few words. He was stoic and constantly in a conversation of fixing or giving me advice. There was nothing gregarious about him. Conversations always seemed to be lessons. There was never time for fairy tales; he read to me from *Tell Me Why*, a book on the science of how things worked. Through my own work I realized that my strategy to be gregarious came from a deep anger and frustration with my father's stoic demeanor.

I had a client whose mom was flighty and undependable. So, her Kid gravitated toward discipline as the strategy of choice. In other cases, clients' parents were stern disciplinarians and their Kids learned that the discipline strategy gained them love, adoration, and great success. But their early childhood decision had a dark side as well.

I've worked with men and women who disciplined themselves so hard—about everything—that their minds and bodies and relationships were breaking down. They had to run more miles, lift more weights, work longer hours. And if they weren't getting the results they were after, well, then they had to run even more miles, lift even heavier weights, and work even longer hours!

That beautiful and productive gift of discipline (that had brought them so much approval) began to destroy their lives and relationships. They took a useful strategy like discipline and began to use it on themselves in a punitive way. The Kid was driving the bus and had his foot on the pedal, which was slammed to the floor. Eventually, the fuel runs out. The bus is on the side of the road.

## THE KING'S WAY

Putting the King in charge is a simple step-by-step process that we'll begin to cover in chapter 5. You'll learn how to put the King in control of fueling and driving the bus. You'll develop the skills and resources the King needs to navigate the road ahead. And we are going to dive much deeper into your new fuel source, the King fuel that will propel you higher and further—with less struggle and more flow. It's not complicated, but it does take some persistence.

Your Kid has been driving the bus for many years, and he isn't about to give up the steering wheel to the King immediately. So, in addition to a step-by-step practice and persistence, you will need something else: courageous inquiry. More than anything, the road ahead will require that you courageously ask questions about and take an in-depth look at the core elements of your behavior and identity. A number of tools and exercises await you to help guide you through this journey.

It can be disorienting when you begin to see just how much your current life, identity, and behavior have been shaped by your Kid. You have to face questions about "Who I am" versus "Who I want to be." It takes courage to start seeing your true being and removing the conditioning—consciously clearing out past experiences' murkiness—so that your Kid is no longer influencing your future. This is your graduation to the King's mindset: discovering what you truly want versus what you've been conditioned to seek.

*At the center of your being*
*you have the answer;*
*you know who you are*
*and you know what you want.*
—LAO TSU

The understanding that so much of who you are is a direct result of your experiences when you were merely a child is critical. Connecting the dots and understanding the relationship that was created in your brain is the key to extending yourself compassion. Ultimately, this is the beginning of the awakening. With that realization comes a new freedom that can also be disorienting. Have you ever seen a caged animal set free in the wild? They often hunker down near the cage, fearful of moving into their new freedom.

TA acknowledges that we were influenced by the expectations and demands of significant others, especially because our early decisions were made at a time in life when we were highly dependent on others. We made certain decisions in order to survive both physically and psychologically at some point in life. The good news is that early decisions can be reviewed and challenged, and if they are no longer serving us, new decisions can be made.

Unconsciously, you've been painting your life on a tiny canvas (no matter how great your current success—believe me—there is far more). As you read on, you'll discover just how large your life canvas is! And, in the next chapter, you will discover another significant source of your inner struggle: your Reaction System. Let's look at that now.

## CHAPTER 3

# Reaction System

I was buried alive....

The small avalanche had come over the rock face and landed on me like a truckload of wet cement.

Darkness.

Silence.

Fear.

I couldn't breathe.

Panic.

Yet moments earlier, I had been enjoying one of the most epic powder days of my life.

So, how did I get here? Here was Alta, Utah, in the mountains high above Rustler Lodge. A group of friends and I caught the last chairlift of the day. We traversed the mountain to an off-piste slope area known as the Eagle's Nest. The view was spectacular: rock faces, trees, untouched powder, and Rustler Lodge nestled just below us.

Each of us picked our own line down the mountain. I launched off a rock face, and as I landed, one of my skis ejected and shot down into the snow. I navigated to a stop on one ski, and then started working my way back to get my other ski. It was brutal. The glorious powder had now turned into my worst enemy as I sunk to my waist with each step. After thirty-five minutes, I'd finally reached the impact point, miraculously found my other ski deep in the snow, and was floundering around trying to get it on.

Just as I locked the ski back on, the ski patrol was doing a last sweep of the mountain, ensuring that everyone had gotten off safely. The patrol, of course, couldn't see me behind the rock face. One of the patrollers set off a small avalanche. I never saw it coming. It launched over the rock face and landed on me like wet concrete. Within seconds, it felt like I was buried alive. Then it swept me down the slope.

I was disoriented, didn't know which way was up or down, didn't have light. I couldn't breathe.

Panic.

After a moment, I figured out I was on my side and thankfully shallow in the snow. I figured out I could pop my head up and gulp air.

Oxygen!

Like this literal avalanche, when we experience emotional avalanches, the amygdala gets highjacked and the Kid takes over. The goal here is to develop presence of mind and become an observer during the real-time event (as the King) so that you can take appropriate action that's consistent with the desired outcome rather than do something that would move you closer to danger. It begins with understanding triggers and reactions.

## TRIGGERS AND REACTIONS

Nothing frustrates us more than the unexpected, bewildering emotional avalanches that sweep through our lives. How can we be so successful and still get hit with emotional avalanches like fear, frustration, anger, procrastination, addiction, self-sabotage, panic, loneliness, overeating, and more? Time and again, clients come to the table with their triggers and frustrations. On the inside all I can hear is "I just don't get it! I'm smart. I've achieved incredible levels of success in my life. What's wrong with me?! Why do I react this way?"

The answer to this question lies in our past: My experience with eye movement desensitization and reprocessing (EMDR) therapy really punctuated for me the connection between my past emotional traumas and how I was experiencing life today. It became abundantly clear that so much of my past experience directly correlated to the emotional triggers I was experiencing as an adult.

Regardless of past successes, we all have emotional triggers and reactions we'd rather avoid. It often feels like we are watching ourselves in a slow-motion movie. We know we shouldn't react a certain way, but here it comes, and we seem powerless to stop it—because our Kid is in control. We know the consequences, but we do it anyway. It is no wonder we go to war with our Kid. Look at the destruction and mayhem he brings into our lives! Fortunately, as I've mentioned, it's possible to change your relationship with your Kid, work with him, and end this internal battle.

> We know the consequences, but we do it anyway. It is no wonder we go to war with our Kid. . . . change your relationship with your Kid, work with him, and end this internal battle.

Before the inner struggle can end, though, you need to understand the source. Two forces work together to create these avalanche trigger-and-reaction patterns in our lives. It's the way we are designed and the inescapable reality of what it is to be human. The first is our hardwired biology, and the second is our early conditioning. Let's take a look.

## A Prehistoric Story

Our modern-day experiences and interactions are being processed through the most primitive part of our brain's limbic system, the amygdala. According to Dr. Joe Dispenza, it is our hardwired reaction system that's responsible for our fight-flight-freeze response. You see, tens of thousands of years ago, the amygdala (or our lizard brain, as it's often called) was responsible for powering that swift kick of adrenaline our ancestors needed to survive. It allowed them to escape whatever terrifying creature was chasing them through the underbrush. To survive, we needed a reaction system that bypassed conscious thought. Our survival demanded a need for pure, instantaneous reaction.

Our homes, offices, and city parks today are generally free from those life-and-death physical threats. But many of us continue to live in a constant emotional state of fight-flight-freeze. We confuse physical survival with emotional survival. The amygdala does not differentiate between real, physical threats and emotional risks. It can't tell the difference between a T-Rex and a partner saying something that threatens our sense of worth. We are not crazy or flawed. The reason we are living in this adrenal-exhausting state is simple human biology. Cue the biology lesson:

Our lungs deliver oxygen to our blood through our respiratory system. Our heart pumps blood through our circulatory system. Our stomach helps break down food to send through our digestive system. And our brain sorts through the billions of pieces of data it receives by running the pieces first through its most antiquated processing system—the amygdala. The brain is continually processing the data it gets through the five senses. As we walk down a busy street, it's scanning the environment for threats. If the amygdala perceives a threat, either physical or emotional, it will react instantly or, as Daniel Goleman called it, get hijacked.

But how does your amygdala judge what's a threat and what isn't? What accounts for one person's lizard brain perceiving a situation as life or death and another seeing the exact same trigger as fun and exhilarating? For example, my friend was hiking with his three-year-old here in Santa Fe, New Mexico. A bullsnake, often confused with a rattlesnake, crossed the path in front of him. My friend's lizard brain reacted instantly, and he swept his son up into his arms as he backed away from the threat. But the three-year-old was enraged and started screaming and squirming to be put down so he could play with the snake. Why did this dad's lizard brain see a threat while his child's brain saw a toy? Enter conditioning.

## Conditioning Lessons

Conditioning is what tells your amygdala what is and isn't a threat. And your conditioning started the day you were born, long before the adult, rational you (the King) had anything to say about it.

### Lesson 1

According to Erikson's model of childhood, when you were born, you came into the world with a built-in response system that would ensure all your survival needs were met. Any discomfort caused you to set off an emergency alarm system that alerted everyone within a two-block radius that you needed something. Hungry? Cry! Dirty diaper? Cry! Uncomfortable onesie? Cry! Your sock fell off? Cry! Want a little more attention? Cry! Your first conditioning lesson was complete: Cry if you feel any discomfort; someone will bring you comfort, love, and nourishment. In Erikson's model, the first phase is all about establishing that type of trust.

### Lesson 2

The second lesson soon followed: If you want to be accepted, fit in with the tribe. As you learned to follow guidelines, established norms, and expectations of the tribe you were born into, your brain was simultaneously programming behavioral response patterns. In the animal kingdom, just as the young watch and learn how their parents hunt and survive for food, we are watching and observing how we can get fed emotionally and be good boys and girls.

This patterned conditioning continues to determine (in almost any situation) the way we interpret, act, and react today. It can be anything from a social event to a board meeting to an argument with our partner to reviewing our child's report card.

This conditioning runs deep. According to Dr. Bruce Lipton, a child's brain is predominantly in the theta-wave state until age seven. Theta waves are the slower waves that enable near subconscious, effortless learning. Messages surrounding our worthiness, lovability, and how we get our needs met all flow into our subconscious mind during this phase of brain development. Between birth and age seven, our mind is absorbing as much information as possible from the external world around us—from our parents, family, community, and teachers. Additionally, Dr. Lipton indicates that this is the time of development when a child's imagination and reality become entangled.

Here's the catch: While we watched, listened, and participated in the activities going on around us, we actually had very little critical consciousness during this phase of development. Our brains simply accepted and did what it could to make sense of these experiences. As a result, the conclusions and decisions we made about the world were often inaccurate.

### Lesson 3

Around age two or three, we are hardwired for another conditioned response—NO! Being hardwired for survival means being able to think and act independently. So, the toddler you started reacting to a lot of the conditioning you were experiencing with a firm "No!"

You struggled to exert your will in a situation over which you had no control. At the very time you were dependent on others for survival, you were also fighting for independence.

"Eat your vegetables."

"No!"

"It's time for bed."

"No!"

"Brush your teeth."

"No!"

Already you see how this hidden inner struggle between your Kid and your King was melded into your existence and at play before you were seven years old!

## Lesson 4

The fourth conditioning lesson we learned as children is "what gets fired together, gets wired together." Here are some examples:

+ A small child got bitten by a dog. Now, as an adult, this person fears man's best friend and will even cross the street to avoid a happy-go-lucky golden retriever.

+ A girl raised her hand in class to answer a question and got it wrong. Her peers mocked her. Now, she's forty-two and hesitant to raise her hand during an executive team meeting.

+ A boy was excited to share a story about his day with his parents, but he was reprimanded for bothering them while they were working. Now, twenty years later, he's hesitant to share important events with his life partner for fear of getting shut down.

In these examples, the amygdala isn't doing the person any favors by drawing snap-judgment conclusions between their early conditioning and current reality. These triggers and patterns that have been wired together by the brain are not accurate matches, but the Kid isn't concerned with accuracy. All three of these past experiences—the biting dog, the wrong answer, and the not-to-be-bothered parents—are considered accurate matches in their present-day Kid mind. I call this Kid logic. **Without exception, my clients underestimate the extent that their past experiences are playing out (and impacting) their decisions as adults.** In the chapters ahead, I'll give you the tools and understanding to respond effectively rather than react automatically.

Kid logic has inappropriate, and unnecessarily dramatic responses on standby for your adult self to react with. Has a situation, circumstance, or argument ever caused you to respond in such a surprising way that you later (or even right in that moment) thought, *Why the hell did I say/do that?* If so, say hello to your Kid in action!

## CONSEQUENCES OF KID LOGIC

If we don't examine our snap assessments, our brain will keep trying to protect us with this unsophisticated mechanism. What was once a valuable part of our brain for physical survival has become obsessed with **emotional survival**. And because this is the conditioned life experience, we need to become aware of how it works. This awareness lets us respond instead of react. It allows us to create our lives through thoughtful responses instead of allowing the Kid's reactions to create them for us. The Emotional Mastery Process, which you will soon start practicing, helps you transform this awareness into life-changing decisions.

There are times when you will be aware that your Kid has suddenly taken control of the bus called your life and driven it into a tree. You know when you have had an emotional avalanche plow through your life and relationships. These battles are the ones that often prompt us to reach out for help because they make us feel guilt and shame and pain. However, we often *don't* recognize the Kid's influence or hear him protesting at all. The Kid's behavior can be most insidious when we aren't consciously aware that he is exerting his influence over our reactions and emotions.

How many times have you had a fleeting idea or dream or goal, and then instantly experience subtle fear and doubt? You dismiss the thought as silly. You never think of it again. For example, as a new author, I struggled with this. I had a strong

> The Kid's behavior can be most insidious when we aren't consciously aware that he is exerting his influence over our reactions and emotions.

desire to write a book, and then the Kid whispered in my ear, "Who do you think you are to try to write a book?" My Kid created the symptoms of self-doubt: cynicism, indecision, and confusion. These were enough to keep me from starting the book and, later, from doing the hard work of turning my manuscript into publishable work. And, as the publishing date drew closer, my Kid did everything he could to prevent me from facing the judgment and criticism of others. My Kid was trying to help me survive emotionally.

Your Kid may simply act in the background, slowly undermining the enthusiasm behind your ideas and robbing you of your initial inspiration and momentum. Once my high-achieving clients come to see how pervasive the Kid's control has been over their reactions, they often have a question: "But in the past, I was always able to battle the Kid's reactions and achieve success. Why am I having such trouble with it now? Why can't I reach the next level just by fighting and disciplining and pure force of will like I used to?" And again, "What's wrong with me?" This often leads to a sudden-onset identity crisis: "Who is this me that can no longer fight and overcome?"

Clients come to realize that the drive and motivation that created their previous success is gone. That motivational fuel has burned out. The fuel they used to drive themselves to high achievement and do battle with the Kid has an expired shelf life. They are shocked to realize that their entire life has been driven by a need to be a good boy or good girl. Confusion sets in as their previous strategy flames out. Decades of chasing status and significance and worth and belonging no longer satisfy—but what to replace it with? Boldness is replaced with hesitation and confusion.

## YOUR TWO CHOICES . . .

You have two choices now:

1. Keep using more discipline, more structure, and more accountability. And if those aren't working, add in more punitive measures to tame your Kid. Wake up every morning and gear up for another battle. Of course, ultimately, this adversarial relationship is unsustainable.

2. Make peace with your Kid. Work with your Kid. And put your King in charge of driving the bus with new, sustainable fuel.

If you are ready for a new, more peaceful relationship with yourself, using an approach you haven't tried before, turn the page.

# CHAPTER 4

# Drop the Sword, Crown the King

He was fighting everyone . . . His political opponents. His family. Himself—especially himself. But that was what he was good at. Fighting and conquering. He was a general. Not only was it what he was good at, but it was his very identity. And it was what he had been rewarded well for his entire life. Only now, the fighting and conquering weren't working anymore. His strategy had expired.

The general was a client of mine. He had transferred from the military into a ministry position in a European country. And now, he found himself under political attack. At the same time, his personal relationships with his wife and kids were at the breaking point. He was also battling some personal demons—and losing.

As we sat in the library at his estate, he stared in contemplation at the fire. In the silence, I watched the fire glint in the droplet sliding down the side of his glass of soda and lime. Finally, he looked at me and asked, "What's wrong with me? Why can't I find a way to beat these damn politicians like I used to? Why can't I crush this thing inside me? Why are my kids turning on me? Why don't I even feel like fighting anymore?"

I told him what I've shared with you: the inner struggle, the duality, between the Kid and the King, the source of it in our early conditioning and biology. I shared with him how the Kid is doing all this for our protection. And then I said, "Right now, this very moment, you are just minutes away from completely changing your relationship with yourself. It can happen in a single moment. Your life can be dramatically better if you can understand one thing. Here it is . . .

"You aren't broken. There is nothing wrong with you. You are simply human. Not one world leader, billionaire, influencer, media personality, or highly accomplished person doesn't, right now, have this hidden inner struggle between their Kid and King robbing them of a better life experience. Their motivational fuel (the Kid fuel of pleasing and being seen and accepted by others) has left them flamed out. And their early conditioning and hardwiring in the amygdala cause them to react in ways that don't live up to their ideals or future goals."

I further explained to him, "The hidden inner struggle between your King and Kid is fierce enough. But you are making it far worse. You don't just react and fight and get triggered. No, you then 'react to the reaction.' You beat yourself up. You criticize yourself worse than any of your enemies. You then experience intense shame and guilt."

He looked away from me and back to the fire. I went on, "And you're still not done with yourself yet. You then react to the reaction of the reaction . . . You take this shame and guilt and disappointment as fuel to punish yourself with harder discipline."

I gave him some common examples of this common human pattern: "If someone breaks their diet, they'll come back with an even stricter diet or cleanse or fast. If someone finds themself procrastinating or wasting time, they'll get accountability coaches to track and account for every minute of their time and punish them when they fall offtrack. General, this is the battle and conquer strategy you've mastered. And, yes, it has brought you great success."

I waved my hand around his estate library. "But it also has both limits and consequences. You see, for all its success, it doesn't bring any sense of lasting inner peace. And it often leaves high achievers like you exhausted and confused. They had the energy for it in their twenties and thirties. But now they ask, 'How many more ladders do I have to keep climbing to ring the success bell?'"

The general looked at me and nodded. "No shit," he said.

I went on, "If you can just come to have compassion on your inner Kid for being human, like everyone else, it can immediately change your relationship with yourself. Replace your anger and frustration and guilt and shame and constant warring with yourself with compassion for yourself."

He raised his eyebrows with skepticism.

I said, "Look, if instead of reacting and fighting at that moment, just have compassion. At that moment, in that space, your King can simply return to the throne—he can take back control of the bus. All the secondary guilt, shame, struggle, and reactions to reactions end. The drama ends."

He looked down at his glass and then raised it to his lips.

I continued, "Even more important, this inner compassion for yourself begins to be reflected outward to others. You already know this: As a leader, you accomplish results through others. That means relationships with others. As your relationship with yourself changes, it starts to change your relationships with your family and those you lead. I realize that me telling you, a general, about leadership may be impertinent. But I can tell you that the leaders I've worked with who begin to give compassion to themselves find themselves naturally extending this compassion to others. And that dramatically alters their experience with their coworkers, teams, partners, spouses, children. Extending compassion creates a better experience. And living a better experience allows you and others to create better results."

The general looked me in the eye. "Not to be blunt, but it sounds too easy to be true."

I said, "General, you have two paths before you. One is the path you are on. Continue fighting yourself, your family, and your political enemies. In fact, you will have to escalate the war and fight harder because what you are doing isn't working. And forgive me for saying this, but what an exhausting way to live. Or you can choose to drop the sword from a position of strength. Give your inner Kid a little compassion. Stop heaping on the self-incrimination and shame and beating yourself into submission. Learn to lead through service. Drop the sword."

The general's eyes squinted; his jaw flexed. I got ready for the angry verbal retort that was coming my way. But then I saw his eyes glistening in the firelight. He squinted his eyes even farther. Then he suddenly got up and left the library. I sat alone in the library, watching the fire, wondering what was going on. After a few minutes, the general's aide came in. The aide said, "In all my years working with the general, I've never seen him get that emotional. I don't know what you said, but it impacted him."

What happened to the general in the months after was remarkable. Much of the anger and sharpness with his staff disappeared. He began leading through service. He began to work with, instead of fighting against, his political opponents. He was reappointed to the ministry.

Now, if like the general, you've reached your current level of success by fighting and warring with yourself, you face the same two paths. Continue struggling to subdue your Kid, or drop the sword and have some compassion for yourself.

DROP THE SWORD, CROWN THE KING

## WHY DO YOU WANT?

There was a time in your life when you didn't criticize yourself and heap shame and guilt on yourself when you let yourself down. In that natural state, you thrived. For example, when you first learned to walk, you often stumbled and fell. When you did, you didn't yell and scream at yourself. You didn't shame yourself: "You idiot! What's wrong with you?!" You didn't set even more aggressive goals: "I will walk a mile by tomorrow!" You just got back up without internal drama and kept trying to walk. There was no emotion attached to it. No judgment. No guilt. No shame.

You see, the misery and suffering start when we heap on the shame and guilt and disappointment of broken expectations. Even though it doesn't seem like it, your Kid isn't being bad but is actually trying to help you survive—physically and emotionally.

Neediness, reactivity, volatility, fear, procrastination, and victim-hood are the hallmarks of the Kid driving your bus. That is because the Kid is guided and ultimately conditioned by the biological fight-flight-freeze response discussed earlier . . . that original source of an infant's cries (a literal fight for survival). Understanding that your inner struggle is your Kid trying to protect you lets you have some compassion for this part of yourself. It lets you return to the natural, nonjudgmental state you once thrived in. And that compassion gives you the space to short-circuit the reactions to the reactions. It gives you the space to put the King back in control of the bus.

The Kid is driven by survival, reaction, and conditioning. The King is driven by purpose, outcomes, and response. Outcomes are revealed by a question, "What do you want?" It's a simple question, yet many struggle to answer it. I've asked over a thousand clients this question, and I see the same patterns repeat.

On one level, clients begin by telling me what they don't want.

"I don't want to be so critical or judgmental." "I don't want to procrastinate so much." "I don't want to blow up important relationships with rage." "I don't want to gain more weight." On another level, they tell me they want the outward symbols of success others have conditioned them to want from childhood. "I want more money, a better car, a home on the water, a more prestigious position."

Scratch beneath the surface on each of these wants, and you discover Kid fuel: They want approval and to be seen by others. Sometimes they get that by being a good boy or girl. Sometimes they achieve it by being a rebel. But the goal remains the same: approval and lovability. They want their emotional cookie.

> **The King does something because he *can* and because it makes *him* happy.**

But there's another level of want. The King's. Ultimately, the King is taking demonstrable action in areas of life that are important to him. The King lives an outcome-driven life. The King does something because he *can* and because it makes *him* happy.

He is not reacting. He's not worried about what others think. He looks into the future and identifies the areas of life that are important to him. He asks, "What is the experience that I'm looking for in each area?" Then he takes action that is consistent with creating that experience.

Living at this outcome-focused level of life, you want what you want—not to please others but because you want to achieve it for yourself. Because it pleases you. No other reasons or excuses or a socially acceptable coat of paint to please others required. I'm going to be honest: This can be disorienting. Discovering that many of your goals, behaviors, and emotions have been driven by the Kid seeking the approval and love of others—or just to survive—can be eye-opening. And while you reorient to *your* true North, there can be a period of disorientation. But soon, you should expect to see dramatic shifts as you reorient to King fuel and your King begins driving the bus.

The inner struggle quiets down. You begin to respond instead of react. Significant relationships are healed. Your experience of life continues to shift as you take steps in the direction of goals and dreams that are *your* goals and dreams. The exhaustion and struggle are replaced with excitement and exhilaration as this new, sustainable fuel fires up. New heights are reached. Your life is reignited.

## SEVEN EFFECTS OF THE EMOTIONAL MASTERY PROCESS

I've mentioned the Emotional Mastery Process several times already, and it's the foundation of this book. I assure you that you'll soon understand exactly what it is. But first I want you to understand the benefits so that you can fully understand why you are doing what I'll be guiding you to do. As I've experienced with my clients, seven things can happen when you use the Emotional Mastery Process:

1. You begin to recognize and understand how and why you feel and react and act in ways that don't serve you. You begin to see common patterns in your life (often from the early life conditioning we discussed in chapters 2 and 3).

2. You experience a different relationship with yourself. You understand that you experience these trigger-reaction chains (aka perception-meaning-feeling-action-outcome chains) because you are human—not because you are inadequate, undisciplined, lazy, or unworthy. This understanding short-circuits the chain reaction of shame and guilt, followed by heaping self-criticism and judgment on yourself, followed by ever more discipline and self-punishment.

3. You begin to anticipate these reactions. You learn the conditions that trigger you. This anticipation allows you to stop the chain reaction before it cascades into a flood of unwanted emotions and behaviors. You spend more and more time as the King with mastery over your emotions.

4. You begin making better decisions. Your mind is calm and clear, as there seems to be more oxygen in the room. You aren't as emotionally frustrated. This lets you see new options and possibilities. And those new paths lead to better life decisions. Your decisions now come from a place of grounded strength and outcomes rather than conditioned reactions.

5. You may pursue new dreams and roads to which you've been blind.

6. You enjoy better personal and professional relationships.

7. You find yourself becoming a better leader. You discover how to extend the compassion and understanding you have given yourself to those you lead in any area of life. You better understand the behaviors and reactions of others and can lead them to focus on outcomes rather than reactive noise.

Nirvana? No. Your Kid has been driving the bus for twenty or thirty or more years. Guess who's not going to like the King driving despite all these positive effects? Your Kid. The reality is this: In a moment of understanding, you can eliminate much of the suffering that comes from secondary reactions. And your inner struggle is reduced when your Kid acts up. But, after a lifetime of conditioning, the Kid will still make appearances. So, you experience both a moment of understanding *and* a lifetime of practice.

*If you could make even just a 10 percent decrease in the amount of time you spend in these Kid-driven negative, stressed, anxious, and triggered states, imagine what that could do for the trajectory of your life.*

## DUALITY IS THE NATURAL ORDER

I'm not sure where humans got the idea that every moment of their lives should be beautiful bliss. I do know that today, more than any time in history, it's shoved in our faces daily on social media. You and I are subjected to a never-ending stream of pictures of everyone else's beautiful life of eternal joy—the toys, the houses, the perfect partners and spouses and children, the world travel, and the well-phrased life purpose they use to signal their value to others.

This life should be perfect dynamic has infected the human race for millennia. But there is no question that it has exponentially multiplied in today's environment. And it is robbing you of joy and having a better life experience. It keeps you from putting your King in charge of the bus and driving it toward what you truly want and desire.

Here's a little dose of truth to help you bridge this gap between expectations, reality, and your possible future. Whoever told you that there would never be setbacks and challenges and "stuff" in your life? There is a day, and there is a night. There are seasons: winter and summer, spring and fall. Because we live in an ever-expanding universe, we will reach these moments of discomfort because we expand right along with it. In nature, a snake sheds its skin. The human body's cells replace themselves every year (you're literally a new person every 365 days!). The immune system gets stronger every time it fights off sickness. This is the yin/yang, the darkness and the light. Duality is inherent in the natural world. We have to come to grips with this in our lives if we want to continue to learn, expand, and grow.

*Experience life in all possible ways—*
*good-bad, bitter-sweet, dark-light,*
*summer-winter. Experience all the dualities.*
*Don't be afraid of experience, because*
*the more experience you have, the more*
*mature you become.*

—OSHO

In my forties, I was living in Encinitas, California. Some of the friends I met there were lifelong surfers. So, I began learning to surf in my forties. The difference between me, the beginner, and my friends, the masters, was eye-opening. I'd see a little wave coming and start paddling like crazy to catch it. Of course, my timing was off, so all that flailing and effort was wasted. Then the next wave would come, and off I'd paddle again. Massive effort. Massive energy. Disappointment. Exhaustion.

My master-level friends had a different experience. As they sat on their boards, they felt the swell, the current. They understood the ocean's patterns and could see and feel a wave coming that I couldn't perceive. And their timing was impeccable. With a few strokes, they caught a beautiful wave. It was near effortless. Then the power of the ocean fueled their ride. With time, I flailed a lot less. I learned which waves to let go of and which to pursue. My timing became better. My experience of surfing went to a completely new level.

Once you understand that your Kid has been dominating your drives and desires and how much inner struggle your battle with the Kid has been creating, you'll understand why you feel exhausted and uncertain about how to move forward. You'll also see that putting the King in charge can bring you a sense of joy. In the next chapter, you'll learn the Emotional Mastery Process, which is one of the fastest ways to put the King back in the driver's seat.

## CHAPTER 5

# The Pathway to Mastery

The archeologists huddled around the computer monitor. What they saw not only shocked them but also changed our understanding of Mayan history. These archeologists had used a new technology called LIDAR (short for Light Detection and Ranging) that let them see below the dense Guatemalan jungle canopy to the ground topography below. And what they saw shattered their expectations. Instead of just a few structures, they saw a vast network of 60,000 structures, dozens of cities, canals, roads and terraces, and infrastructure.

It was immediately apparent that the Mayan Empire was not a disjointed group of city-states but a vast, networked, sophisticated empire with a population of over 10 million people! This new understanding was all made possible by a new tool: LIDAR. Just as the telescope and microscope enabled discoveries that weren't possible before, this new tool, LIDAR, made it possible to see a world we didn't know existed.

Bottom line: New tools that extend our senses enrich our insights and understanding of the world. And I want to share a tool with you that will change your world: the Emotional Mastery Process (EMP). **EMP is the missing link: the space between stimulus and response**

**that creates life mastery.** This process allows you to see (often for the first time) insights and patterns into the battle between your Kid and King. EMP helps you achieve emotional and life mastery by slowing down your automatic reaction process to life's triggers and then using the triggers as a catalyst for personal growth and mastery.

## THE TREASURE MAP

Intense triggers are a treasure map to personal growth and inner riches. Let me explain it with a personal story: Even though my parents were from India, my family wasn't very religious. My dad's belief was that religion was the opiate of the masses. Education is what's important. So, as a young kid when I traveled to India to visit my grandfather every summer, I became intrigued by all the deities, especially those of Jainism and its philosophy, which was deeply rooted in our family. But of all the deities that I was exposed to, the one that captured my attention most was the elephant-headed god, Ganesh.

I learned that Ganesh was the remover of obstacles. As a kid, that fascinated me because I seemed to have trouble all the time. My life seemed like one perpetual obstacle. So, I was drawn to the idea of Ganesh. And I wasn't alone. Hindus, Buddhists, Muslims, and Jains all agree on Ganesh.

On the surface, he is just about luck—a lucky charm for Indians. Even in my nonreligious family, we still have a tradition of handing out silver Ganesh coins to celebrate certain life events. It wasn't until later in life that I understood the deeper meaning of Ganesh. I was surprised to learn that Ganesh didn't just help remove obstacles, but he actually placed obstacles in our path for growth.

Most people believe they just need to invoke Ganesh to remove their obstacles. They don't recognize that he won't give them a barrier-free life. That's not what Ganesh is there for. He's there to help you meet the obstacle that comes and form a new relationship with it. The block is an opportunity for something to be learned and transcended in your human form right now. Whenever we experience intense negative emotions, they result from a perceived obstacle that "shouldn't be that way." An obstacle (often a person) prevents us from achieving something we believe we want, need, and desire. That obstacle leads then to an emotional reaction:

"I'm frustrated."

"I'm sad."

"I'm confused."

"I'm uncertain."

"I don't have clarity."

Those emotional reactions can either lead you down a path to self-blame, doubt, despair, and poor decisions or they can be the doorway to the treasures of personal growth, powerful decisions, and a richer life experience. Fact: The more we can transcend our obstacles, the better experience we can have in our life. The opportunity to have a great experience in life is rooted in the number of obstacles we can meet head-on, change our relationship with, understand, and put into proper context. This is how we grow and learn. This is how we reach the next levels in our life. Transcending obstacles is the pathway of the King. When we observe obstacles in this way, we can say, "Yes, that was awesome. I wonder when the next opportunity to grow is?"

As Jiddu Krishnamurti said in *Think on These Things*:

> *Intelligence is the capacity to perceive the essential . . . the what is. It is only when the mind is free from the old that it meets everything new . . . and in that there's joy. To awaken this capacity in oneself and in others is real education.*

## THE EMOTIONAL MASTERY PROCESS

How do we transform from a Kid who just reacts to events and emotions into a King who uses the obstacles to reach new levels of significance and fulfillment? The Emotional Mastery Process uses five simple questions (the 5 EMP Questions) to put your King back in the driver's seat. The catalyst to use these five questions is any time your experience of life is not what you want it to be. The following is an overview of the questions. We will dive into each one individually in the following chapters. It starts with learning to be a nonjudgmental observer.

### ■ EMP QUESTION 1: What did I observe? What *really* happened?

What we think happened often didn't. As you learn more about the implications of this simple question, you'll realize just how much of your past conditioning is coloring your present experience. This question will be eye-opening. As you master this question, you will learn to describe the facts in your life without the judgments that often distort our view of reality.

> *To come upon truth the mind must be*
> *completely free, without a spot of distortion.*
> —JIDDU KRISHNAMURTI, *FREEDOM FROM THE KNOWN*

### ■ EMP QUESTION 2: What did I conclude?

Rarely is an event of any kind just an experience. We are wired to understand what we are experiencing by our conditioned past experience and we are wired to jump to conclusions. In this step of the process, you'll begin to untangle your observations with your interpretation. And you'll see how the conditioning of your past experiences is impacting how you're experiencing the actual event.

## ■ EMP QUESTION 3: Based on my conclusion, what was my emotional state?

Your feelings flow directly from the conclusions you reach about the events that you observe. And you will discover repeating patterns of triggers-meaning-feeling during this step of the process. While these interpretations we give to events create our feelings, it's the feelings that drive our actions and behaviors. Simply put, developing mastery over your emotions will change where you end up in life.

## ■ EMP QUESTION 4: What action did I take from that emotional state?

Broadly, there are three actions the Kid takes in response to feelings: fight, flight, or freeze. But these reactions break into common behavior patterns that sell a lot of self-help books:

+ Procrastination

+ Overworking

+ Anger

+ Coping mechanisms like drugs, alcohol, and porn

+ Binge-watching TV

+ Extreme dieting

+ Showing off

+ Self-criticism

The fourth question gives you deep insight into how you quickly jump to conclusions and ultimately react.

# ■ EMP QUESTION 5: Did that action move me closer to or further away from my intended outcome?

Now you arrive at the King's question. The King is outcome driven. The King takes actions toward objectives that are important and meaningful to him. The King learns to discern between Kid-driven, reactive, conditioned outcomes and outcomes he wants to pursue because they are meaningful to him.

These 5 EMP Questions are your LIDAR to seeing the root causes of your life's experience. They will provide you with life-changing distinctions and help you make better decisions from which your life flows.

Now obviously, the time to run yourself through these questions is after an event has triggered you—not in the heat of the moment. The Emotional Mastery Process is an "after-action" tool. Away from the heat of the moment, you take the time to work through the invisible perception-meaning-feeling-action-outcome chains. You begin to understand why you felt the way you did, decided on the actions you did, and received the outcomes you did. If you get nothing else from this book other than practicing these five questions whenever you are triggered, you will still dramatically transform your life!

## SLOW-MOTION MAGIC

When I taught skiing, the hardest students to work with were intermediate skiers. That's because, by the time they had reached the intermediate level, many of their bad habits actually felt right to them. And, ironically, the corrections I gave them felt wrong. It wasn't uncommon for them to hear a correction, go back to doing it habitually wrong, and then think they had made the correction.

The magic solution to this problem was video recording. I would record them and then play it back. Now they could see for themselves the mistakes they were making. But even that wasn't good enough to bring about change. I had to go a step further and put the video in slow motion so they could see smaller distinctions they could take action on. For example, take the ski turn. At full speed, a turn looks like a single skill element. But there are actually three parts to it: the initiation, the fall line, and the finish. Then each of those elements has smaller distinctions. That's the level where the skier can make changes that transform their turns.

The same is true with our triggers. There are five elements of a trigger. But without slowing them down with the 5 EMP Questions, you'll never see them or their more subtle distinctions. It will just seem like a single angry reaction or moment of hurt. And that really doesn't give you anything meaningful to change.

Typically, the strong, athletic skiers had the hardest time. They had the strength to muscle through turns and wrestle themselves down the hill. So what if they had to work ten times harder than a more efficient skier; it was working for them, so why change? They were in for a rude awakening in their forties and fifties: Years of working against the forces of nature, like gravity and momentum, left them with knee and ankle injuries. Age slowly took away their strength. Their strategy wasn't sustainable. This is very much like many high achievers. They have the emotional strength to battle the Kid into submission, so why do anything differently? Like skiers who muscled through, their strategy isn't sustainable either.

It is so much easier and elegant to work with the forces of nature. You can ski all day and not become exhausted. You have a more enjoyable experience. And, frankly, you're more pleasing to be around and watch as you navigate the slope with grace and elegance. The same is true in your life. When you use the 5 EMP Questions (like a slow-motion video replay) to review your emotional triggers, it's a total game changer. You begin to realize with each question that there is a world of possibilities and options you had never realized before. You now understand the chains of reaction that led to undesirable actions. And you perceive the myriad of possible perceptions, meanings, feelings, responses, and outcomes available to you at each link in the chain.

It's like following a tree trunk up to its ever-expanding branches—each leading to a different potential reality. Of course, you'll still have emotional reactions to people and events that surprise and disappoint you. Yes, you're human . . . None of us get to avoid being human. Your heart pumps blood. Your lungs bring oxygen. Your mind creates chains of perception-reaction outcomes. But we can understand why we often react in ways we don't want to. We can decrease the intensity and duration of our trigger-reaction chains when we do. And we can learn to anticipate and neutralize them before they start. The Emotional Mastery Process is the road map to accomplishing that. With practice, you'll be able to

1. Reduce the intensity with which you experience negative emotions.

2. Reduce the time you feel these negative emotions.

3. Learn to see reactions coming and just let them pass like a wave.

4. Improve your working and personal relationships.

5. Improve your leadership skills.

6. Create a much better life.

7. See possibilities and potential for your life and future that you can't imagine right now.

8. End much of the adversarial relationship between the Kid and the King and come to a more loving and compassionate view of yourself and others.

In the next chapter, you'll see how pervasive our conditioned perception-meaning-feeling-action-outcome chains can be even in everyday encounters, and you'll have the opportunity to experience the 5 EMP Questions in action. Later, we'll take a deep dive into each link in the chain.

# CHAPTER 6

# The Emotional Mastery Process at Work

In early 2000, I was leading a small group at a seminar being held at a hotel. The hotel had only two restaurants to serve about 1,500 participants. We had only an hour to eat and complete an exercise in our lunch group. We waited in line for five minutes to get seated. And once seated, we waited . . . and waited.

As everyone was anxiously mulling over how much time was passing with no waiter in view, a young man silently dropped some bread on the table and hurried off.

My friend Caroline got visibly angry. "I'm getting the manager. This place doesn't have its shit together, and we've only got an hour for lunch!"

"Hang on," I suggested. "Before we go there, does anyone have a different take on this?"

Kerri quickly chimed in, "Maybe the waiter is just having a bad day. Let's send him some good energy and turn this around."

Meanwhile, having worked in the restaurant business myself and observing the crowd the waiters were trying to handle, I was happy to have received some bread. As we discussed the pros and cons of giving the guy a chance or calling the manager over, the same young man came over to introduce himself.

"Hi, my name is Chris, and I'll be taking care of you today. Hopefully, you've had a chance to look over the menus while enjoying some bread. The chef knows you're on a time crunch, and we should be able to get you out in twenty-five minutes. Would that be okay?"

This young man was awesome, energetic, and personable. We had a great meal and learned about Chris's plan to go to law school to become an immigration lawyer. We ended up leaving him a 30 percent tip and walked out of there with our assignments completed and our bellies full.

## EXPLORING THE 5 EMP QUESTIONS

Let's use the restaurant scenario to explore the 5 EMP Questions from my perspective to help you really understand the gist of the questions:

**EMP Question 1:** What did you observe? Just the facts, please.

Think about the incident. Try to separate what actually happened from the embellishments and opinions. You want to think of it as if you were filling out an official accident report. Just think of the specifics. Leave the emotions out of it.

In this case: *"We waited for five minutes to get into a restaurant. Upon being seated, we waited five minutes before a man put bread on our table and walked away."* Notice how I stripped this statement of any interpretation. Was the restaurant busy? Crowded? Was the man our waiter? At the time, we didn't know. We didn't even know if he was a restaurant employee. It's critical to separate opinions and interpretations from actual facts.

**EMP Question 2:** What did you conclude from your observations?

Caroline concluded that the restaurant was unorganized and unprofessional. She believed that she wouldn't be able to eat and get our group assignment done on time. She thought that our waiter was disrespectful and didn't care about our needs.

Kerri figured the guy was just having a bad day. He may have been stressed. He may have been overwhelmed because we all came in at once. She thought that it was unfair for the waiter to have so many tables at once. Kerri was also responding to Caroline's desire to go to the manager and concluded that we were about to make a scene.

Yes, we could reasonably argue that it would have been nice for the young man who dropped the bread to say: "I'll be right with you." Other than that, we made up stories based on our perception.

Take a moment now to understand how much opinion gets mixed in when we describe anything that we observe.

**EMP Question 3:** What feeling resulted from your conclusion? What emotional state did you experience?

In Caroline's case, because she concluded something negative, she went straight to frustration and anger. In Kerri's case, she went to compassion for the waiter as well as her conditioned fear. And that led to her avoidance and peacekeeping in response to Caroline's reaction.

**EMP Question 4:** What action did you take as a result of that emotional state?

In our case, we didn't do anything, as Chris, the waiter, came back quickly to take our order. But how might this have played out if we had acted on our emotional response?

If left unchallenged, Caroline would have risen in an emotional state of anger and frustration and demanded to speak to the manager. A good manager might have calmed her and expedited the order. But the tension created by Caroline's triggered self would probably have lingered through the meal.

Left to her own devices, Kerri would have tried to engage Chris, sending him good positive vibes. She would have asked him how he was doing and if he was having a good day. She would have probably slowed him down, letting her concern for his (fabricated) bad day interfere with his work because she was worried about him.

The rest of us just watched. We could have done something or not, but realize that both action and inaction can be outcomes of our responses to Question 2.

**EMP Question 5:** Did that action move you closer to or further away from your intended outcome?

This is actually a tricky question and probably the one that is most important for you to get clarity around. We could also ask the bonus question: "What was your intended outcome in the first place?" Let's look more deeply at this question now.

## Outcomes versus Expectations

Most people in these situations have unspoken expectations as opposed to intended, desired outcomes. I'll go further . . . The single greatest cause of unhappiness and disagreements I witness is this: People have unspoken expectations rather than clearly defined outcomes.

> **The single greatest cause of unhappiness and disagreements I witness is this: People have unspoken expectations rather than clearly defined outcomes.**

We go in with unconscious expectations of how people, places, and things should be according to our projected model of the world. We are directors of our own stage show and get frustrated with our cast of supporting characters for not following a script they have never seen.

Before lunch, no one said, "Hey, let's take a moment to think about the kind of experience we want to have." Instead, we rolled out of our seminar, expecting to eat something and to complete our assignment. We expected to get our task accomplished and did not think much at all about the experience outcome. We could have set an intention for a calm, relaxed, and focused lunch. Seeing that there was a line and the restaurant looked busy, we could have decided to appreciate the staff for doing their best during such a crowded lunch hour.

Think about how many situations you walk into with an unspoken expectation rather than a clear outcome. But by pursuing a desired outcome, you are free to navigate a changing world—and enlist the aid of the people around you. On the other hand, defending your expectations creates an endless parade of problems and frustrations. How many unnecessary arguments have we gotten into with our loved ones and coworkers? How much unnecessary suffering have we put on ourselves and others because of unwritten expectations that we held ourselves and others responsible for?

Here's the most amazing thing about this restaurant experience. The reality was this: We walked into a restaurant, waited for five minutes, got bread, and were met with an energetic waiter who provided excellent service, terrific food, and got us out of the restaurant with plenty of time to spare. Chris was engaging, professional, and was, in fact, having a great day meeting all kinds of interesting people. He was stoked to have a job that would fund his mission to help immigrants. The back of the house was totally prepared and was able to deliver high-quality food that was presented professionally in a timely fashion.

Caroline wasn't able to follow through on her reaction because the restaurant actually had its act together. The action of a man putting bread on our table triggered Caroline. It created an emotional state of frustration and anger. From that place, she might have created an angry scene. I could even argue that she would have gotten her desired outcome—she would have been served, and we would have completed our assignment.

Would Chris have been as enthusiastic? Probably not. Chris would most likely have been apologetic and less energetic. We almost certainly would not have heard about his plans for law school. The manager might have tried to make us feel better by buying us dessert or comping our meal. Still, Caroline's action would have created a tense and argumentative situation that would have dampened our experience unnecessarily.

What's worse is that if we had let Caroline continue with her intended action to speak to the manager, it would have reinforced that behavioral pattern within her. Anytime she doesn't feel acknowledged, she gets mad and demands immediate action. Here's the irony. Caroline would have gotten someone to take action by raising hell at the table. It would have reinforced her belief that it was the only way to get what she wanted. And I'm not picking on Caroline; we ALL do this.

We rob ourselves of experiences, people, and opportunities because we are continually triggered. We are using invalid strategies without knowing the spoken or unspoken consequences of our actions.

Many of the leaders I train think of themselves as great leaders because they have the respect of their management teams. While these leaders get good work from their managers, they leave untapped potential on the table. Innovation and creativity in organizations are killed with this kind of approach. This is a classic pattern that gets wired together, becoming part of the permanent company culture.

Think about how much low-hanging fruit we miss because we either live in fear or we miss opportunities. When we allow our Kid to hijack our bus, we're shutting doors to new opportunities because we feel we have to protect ourselves. We've lost our innate curiosity about the world around us. Instead of asking questions, we choose to live in preconceived notions that are easier to deal with than the act of creating a disruption (aka discomfort) with new information.

When we're not engaged, we're also not leading with compassion and love. We just presume we know the answers, so we stop asking questions, and we miss out. The actions we take as a result of our interpretations are directly related to the emotional state that has been created by that same interpretation. If we want to claim our power and step into our Kingliness, we must develop personal mastery of our triggers.

Let's take a look at this event using the knowledge you gained in chapters 2 and 3 about early life conditioning and hardwiring.

## What Was Up with Caroline?

Caroline was the middle child of three and often felt ignored. Her significantly older sister was an alcoholic, and much of her teenage years were spent helping raise her younger sister. At the same time, her parents focused on her older one. She never felt her needs were met because her older sister's behavior dominated the house.

Today, Caroline's car, body, hair, makeup, purse, clothes, and shoes personify the statement: "You will notice me . . . and I will not be ignored." She would argue that her personality serves both her career and her clients well, and is a great deal of the reason she is so successful. In fact, clients hire her for her aggressive "get it done" approach. She didn't feel taken seriously, so she channeled that frustration into a career as an attorney and became a fierce advocate for her clients.

Since her Kid was ignored, that's who showed up at the restaurant when Caroline felt ignored. Not being noticed as a child triggered anxiety and fear. As an adult, it translated into anger. And that anger would have created a reaction that would have robbed her of a pleasant experience at lunch. Her actions could have affected everyone in the restaurant, our table, our waiter, and the manager. And all because her Kid showed up to protect her from being ignored.

Through coaching, Caroline maintained that it would have been better for the waiter to have acknowledged the table. Still, she also understood that she was triggered. Caroline recognized her emotional reaction. From that state, she was not as effective at communicating as she might have been. She was actually shocked to see how directly the situation at the restaurant correlated with her childhood history of being ignored!

Just getting this one concept has changed her approach to just about every situation she has encountered since; this pattern was affecting her in more ways than one. She has begun to notice when she is triggered and responds instead of just reacting. The result: she's just a lot more pleasant and happier these days.

We underestimate the power that our experiences of the past have on our lives today. Because of her experience with her sister at a young age, Caroline learned that she has a propensity to go to feeling ignored more easily than most. This was a significant part of her childhood experience. No matter how much awareness and how much work she does, she will get triggered.

Caroline and I worked through the 5 EMP Questions together on an ongoing basis. Over time, we recognized the circumstances and personality types that would trigger her. Eventually, she could anticipate the trigger and quickly put her Queen back in the driver's seat so that she could get the outcome she wanted. We also spent time figuring out not only the external circumstances but also the internal circumstances that triggered her. It came down to having her life in order. If things were out of alignment (her finances, health, fitness, or any part of her life), she was more prone to getting triggered.

After some time, we developed a preventative pathway to mitigate the frequency, intensity, and duration of any trigger and also identified a quick path to get her back on track.

## What about Kerri?

How about Kerri? Kerri grew up with an alcoholic dad. She told me stories about hiding under her bed with her sister when her father started drinking because she knew what was coming next. The more her father drank, the angrier he became. He would yell at her mother and break things.

She and her sister knew they were powerless to stop it. Her survival mechanism was to flee (the flight response) because a confrontation with her father was out of the question. As an adult, Kerri liked to appease situations to keep everything calm—she was a master of conflict avoidance. Kerri was incredibly attuned to reading people because her survival as a kid depended on it. So at the restaurant, she observed what she thought was a stressed-out waiter about to get in trouble when Caroline threatened to call the manager. At this, her Kid took over and began working to appease the situation.

As an adult Kerri is an amazing interior designer who creates beautiful spaces for her clients. Before doing these exercises, her incredible talent was locked behind the instinct of playing it safe. Once she was free from this reactionary pattern, she was finally free to grow her business to its fullest potential.

## The Group Reaction

Now let's talk about the group that didn't speak up at that restaurant. What if, because of Caroline's reaction, the rest of us decided to just get up from the table and sit somewhere else? That would be a flight thing to do for sure. And don't think some of us didn't consider it. But in the end, our reaction was to just sit silently without verbalizing any discomfort or desire. This is an example of freezing when a trigger circumstance arises.

Many people with conflict-avoiding personalities will freeze or flee. Unfortunately, I see this conflict avoidance behavior quite a bit in organizations. All it takes is an employee feeling unseen, unheard, shut down, ignored, or belittled—and he or she may stop bringing new ideas to the table. And managers who want to be liked will end up tolerating behavior that eventually becomes problematic. Their need to be liked and not create conflict creates greater problems for them and their organizations.

At the restaurant that day, the rest of us just watched Caroline overreact because we didn't want to cause a scene. We sat there at the table complaining to ourselves that her reaction was excessive but not saying anything. In essence, we clammed up in freeze mode while allowing the uncomfortable situation to persist.

What would you say is your conditioned, predominant reaction to fear and discomfort: fight, flight, or freeze? How does this present itself when you are triggered? In the next chapters, we will do a deep dive into the first of the 5 EMP Questions.

# CHAPTER 7

# Perception versus Reality

"Watch out!" I shouted to my students.

A reckless skier in camouflage gear flew past my group, made an unfortunate turn, and shot deep into the trees. Tragically, he hit one of the trees at high velocity. I'd had my eye on this guy for a while. He was a classic case of an inexperienced skier with a big ego skiing beyond his limits. A "hold my beer" kind of guy. I first noticed him when he came off the ski lift. It was hard not to. He had crossed his skis and fallen on his face in the snow. That caused the lift to stop while he crawled out of the way. Later, he was skiing at high speeds on the slope through packed holiday weekend crowds.

I sent my students to get the ski patrol while I went into the trees to help him. As the first person on the scene, it was my job to stay with him throughout the rescue. I did my best to stabilize him while waiting for the patrol. I stayed with him down the slope. I was with him when they loaded him on the helicopter. By the time I returned to the patrol offices, it had been a long day. I was emotionally devastated and physically exhausted. Adrenaline had fueled me for over half the day. Part of me felt guilty for having judged the guy and part of me was just pissed off at the whole situation.

I thought I was done for the day and ready for a beer when all of a sudden . . . I got to do all the paperwork. It was here I learned a lesson that I've carried with me ever since. As I was filling out the incident report, there was a simple question: What happened? I filled out the information and handed it to my supervisor.

He read it over and handed it back. "How do you know he was a beginning skier? How do you know he had a big ego? Were you inside his mind? How do you know the exact speed he was skiing? How do you know he made a bad turn—maybe he had a heart attack and passed out. How do you know he was over his skill level on the slope? What does it matter if he was wearing camouflage?" And on it went.

It turns out that when millions of dollars in liability are at stake, my language mattered a lot. Lawyers in court will attack any interpretation or misunderstanding of the facts. Lawyers and their clients just can't get this wrong. It's that important. I was forced to strip down the event to observable facts. No embellishment. No interpretations based on my past experience and opinions. No biases based on how the skier was dressed.

This was thirty years ago, but I believe that the final statement I wrote was "A man skied past me, turned off the slope, and hit a tree. He was unconscious when I reached him." Gone were all my interpretations and biases based on how he was dressed and acting.

That singular life lesson thirty years ago drilled into my mind that many of the things I "thought" I observed, I didn't. Many things I thought were the truth weren't. All of us cloud our mind with the fog of the past, mix it with our biases and beliefs, and then serve it to ourselves and others as the truth. This event had a major impact on both my life and my work with clients.

So, what did you observe? Such a simple question. And so hard to answer. This is critical: It's not just millions of dollars you have at stake. Your quality of life, your future is at stake every time you layer perceptions and interpretations on top of a life event. When your enjoyment of life is at stake, preciseness is important. The distinctions are important. Every detail is important. It is critical that we begin to treat our lives this way!

> *Reality is merely an illusion, albeit a very persistent one.*
> —ALBERT EINSTEIN

The 5 EMP Questions show you the distinct mechanics of what has been stopping you from living a life you love. That's why this first question, "What did you observe?" is the master key to set yourself free and reach new heights of achievement, to see and seize opportunities, and to create a better relationship with yourself and others. It provides a moment of nonjudgment when you are free to choose a new path toward a renewed, reignited life.

## THE MASTER KEY

Mastering this moment of nonjudgment is the key to mastering your life and its rich possibilities. Our perception of reality is the first link in the perception-interpretation-feeling-action-outcome chain. So, it's critical we are clear on what is really happening—all our experience cascades from this first link.

Science tells us that perception is not reality. Our perceptions of reality are easily tricked by optical illusions and misperceptions. Even nature uses perceptual sleight of hand. Take the color red, for instance. Nature often gives that color to dangerous things. The red hourglass on a black widow. The red rings of a lethal coral snake. Every spring here in Santa Fe, New Mexico, the hummingbirds migrate instinctually to the multitude of feeders that I put up every season. At the height of the season, it is not uncommon to see twenty to thirty at a time! Occasionally, a male perceives me as a threat. This tiny creature will fly up toward my face aggressively and flash his brilliant, iridescent red throat feathers. He's trying to trick my perceptions into believing he's a dangerous threat.

Numerous experiments show that experienced wine experts can be fooled by the bottle and label wine is poured from. Cheap wine in an expensive bottle tastes expensive. Chefs know that how food is plated impacts our perceptions of how great it tastes. And marketing experts know that product and package design have a profitable effect on our perceptions of quality and value. Associations affect our perception of reality. If you want to sell a luxury automobile, hire a famous actor, put them in a tux, and have them drive it into a mansion's circular driveway.

Expectations can also alter how we perceive reality. For example, in one experiment, subjects were shown an object that is usually hot but was actually ice cold. When the object touched the subjects' skin, the subjects felt like they were being burned. Maybe this has happened to you. You are warming up the water. You stick your hand in the stream to test it. It scalds you. Only moments later, you discover you accidentally turned the knob to cold instead of hot.

The events immediately before an experience can dramatically influence our perceptions of reality. If it is a boiling hot day, jumping into a warm pool can make it seem like the water is cold. Yet, if it's a cold, overcast day, the same water feels like a warm bath.

Even the setting an event happens in can bend our perception of reality. A high-end jeweler would never show you an expensive diamond pendant by laying it on a clear glass display case. Instead, he would pull out a black velvet cloth, gently unroll it, and then carefully place the pendant on it. The contrast between the black background and brilliant stone makes it appear even more vibrant—and expensive.

One of the most influential creators of our expectations, associations, and experiences was our early life—the Kid's life. This never ceases to surprise my clients. They begin to understand the power of expectations, beliefs, associations, and conditioning that happened when they were five or seven or ten years old.

I give you all these examples to help you understand just how relative and untrustworthy our observations can be. This simple question gives our King's wisdom the time to suspend the Kid's knee-jerk reactions to perceived emotional threats and stop him from jumping to conclusions that don't serve him. Additionally, it also allows us to have compassion for ourselves for being human—rather than beating ourselves up with guilt and shame. We are experiencing the same misperceptions of reality every other human on the planet is having! Now it's your turn to practice this first question: What did you observe? What *really* happened?

## PRACTICE: EMP QUESTION 1—
## What did I observe? What *really* happened?

1. **Pick a moment.** Think of a recent experience that was emotionally charged, one where your Kid was definitely driving the bus. Maybe a fight with a spouse or partner, a heated disagreement at work, or a political debate with a family member or friend. Choose something that really set you off and was high on the emotional intensity and duration scale.

2. **Write out what you observed.** Write up an accident report as though it was an official document. No embellishments. Just write the specifics. Include no emotion or feelings about the circumstances. Just the facts.

_____

_____

_____

3. **Scrub it.** Separate opinions and interpretations from your observations. Omit adverbs and adjectives; these words are laden with judgment. Think like a journalist for a moment: Who, what, when, where, and why? Note who was there and what was said. Don't get hung up on the meaning of others' comments; just state them as best you can. Now rewrite your description scrubbed of all adjectives, adverbs, opinions, judgments, and guesses about what the other person meant or was thinking (aka mind reading).

_____

_____

_____

4. **Take a final scan.** Scan the document one last time to make sure it is interpretation free. Does it leave room for the opposing person or group to agree to the facts?

Congratulations! You've just taken the first step on the pathway to mastery and at the very least prepped to fill out your first accident report. ☺ You are beginning to reveal the invisible bars of past conditioning that keep you from experiencing life at a more profound level. In fact, this first step gives you an advantage over 99 percent of the population who never learn to adopt the observer role—those who don't dare question their interpretation of events. The next chapter examines how quickly and how often you jump to conclusions.

CHAPTER 8

# Things Are Not Always What They Seem

Samantha brought her hands to her face, covering her eyes. Tears were streaming down her face. She ran out of the manager's office and into the restroom. The office was one of those all-glass, modern cubes. Everyone could see in but couldn't hear the conversation.

From his desk, Sam saw it happen. He felt awful that Samantha had been fired. In fact, he'd been working up the nerve to ask her out.

Susan, who had also witnessed the scene, was incensed. This manager was an authoritative, patriarchal pig, and he always promoted pretty women whether or not they had any skills. Susan had already been passed over for promotion twice this year—and now Samantha had just gotten a promotion after working there only two months; what's worse, she even dared cry tears of joy! Susan stormed off to HR.

Steve had watched as well. He felt awful for Samantha. He remembered when he'd been called in to the manager's office and was told that his mom had been in an accident. His family had been trying to call him, but he'd accidentally left his phone home that day. He wiped a tear from his cheek.

Savannah was walking back to her desk when she saw Samantha run from the manager's office. Savannah was angry. Their manager tended to criticize even the smallest mistakes. She thought it was a wonder that he was ever given a leadership role. Just last week, he had criticized her ad design because he didn't like the shade of blue she had chosen.

The manager in the glass office got up to refill his coffee. *Well, that was a first,* he thought. He and Samantha had been discussing the company picnic when she brought her hand to her eye. She tried to continue the conversation, but then said the pain was horrible. She thought maybe her contact had torn. With her hand over her eye and tears streaking down her cheeks, she ran out of the office.

As Malcom Gladwell discussed in his book *Blink*, you and I, as humans, are wired to interpret the world from the events we experience. In a fraction of a second, we judge an event good or bad, right or wrong, dangerous or safe. Our ability to create snap judgments is part of our hardwiring and exists for our survival. It's so automatic that many of us don't realize just how much control we have over the meanings we create. We think they just are. But as the office example shows, any single event can have different meanings based on who's experiencing it. There are 7.6 billion people in the world. And there are 7.6 billion different points of view and opinions that get created around any given event.

## IT'S ALL RELATIVE

Our ability to make snap judgments is a gift from nature that helps us survive. When lions, tigers, and cobras were part of our daily existence, we needed to quickly assess what was dangerous or safe. In today's world, our minute by minute survival is usually not at stake. But our emotional survival is. And our Kid is the protector of our emotional survival. Our Kid wants to be loved and feel worthy and be comfortable. If anything threatens that, the Kid is going to form an opinion about it. He'll judge it as unfair, unjust, and dangerous. And then all those feelings of unworthiness and feeling unloved, isolated, angry, frustrated, and incensed flow from that meaning and into decisions and actions that don't serve a fulfilling life.

The King needs to be in control of our judgment faculties. And step one in this context is fully understanding that it's all relative. We are continually shaping it based on all the conditioning and patterning and experiences from day to day going back to when we were young. The next step is realizing that developing mastery in managing the knee-jerk conclusions we come to is one of the most significant levers to a more fulfilled life. If we learn to master this, we can stop the cascade of toxic feelings and actions that flow and intensify downstream. Want to feel better? Want to experience a happier, more enjoyable life? Then you want to put the King in charge and let him take the lead.

> In today's world, our minute by minute survival is usually not at stake. But our emotional survival is.

Emotional mastery is not about living with an absence of an opinion or having a perspective. It's not even about changing your point of view. It's first and foremost understanding and accepting that you *are wired to interpret the data you gather from your five senses.* And you will have emotional reactions to the knee-jerk reactions of your mind. It's the acknowledgment that nothing actually *is* anything or a particular way. Your reality is not a reality; it's a perceived reality that's unique to you. Yes, while you might find a consensus of belief, I can guarantee that I can find someone who would challenge your very notion of what you think is your truth. One of the most beautiful wedding vows I heard years ago was "I promise to never know you." It took everyone aback at first, but the groom went on to explain that he always wanted to discover something new about his wife every day, to treat her as a dynamic, growing, and evolving partner. How often have we put people in a box? "He is this . . ." "She is that . . ." (Heck, I did that with my father for years, which you will read about later.)

Life becomes so much more peaceful when we realize that our perception creates our reality. Yes, we will experience events, automatically jump to conclusions, have strong feelings, and sometimes react in ways we didn't want to. It's human nature. Stopping the secondary reactions of self-criticism, shame, and guilt for doing what every human is hardwired to do creates even more peace.

Emotional mastery is about understanding that many of these perception-meaning-feeling-action-outcome chains have become automatic-reaction chains that are keeping you from a better quality of life. They have become unsustainable, self-limiting patterns that are actually quite predictable. Yes, perhaps they worked early in your life. But now, for your future self, your future relationships, and your future achievements, you must learn to identify, anticipate, and interrupt the automatic chain so that you can powerfully choose an action consistent with your chosen outcomes. When you understand how these patterns are created, it takes you a long way on the journey to achieving emotional mastery in your life.

> **Identify, anticipate, and interrupt the automatic chain so that you can powerfully choose an action consistent with your chosen outcomes.**

## The Kid's Influence on How You Experience the World

As in the story of the office workers, much of how you experience life comes from your personal history, experiences, and conditioning. A simple example of this is the weather. Say it's sixty degrees and sunny outside. If you are from Colorado, that means it's time for shorts and you and ditch the jacket. If you're from California, it's time to consider wearing long pants and your winter coat! Your decision to wear long pants is conditioned by your previous experience.

As we discussed earlier, the conditioning you experienced as a kid has some of the most profound influences on how you experience life today. Learning your Kid's unique patterns of triggers and reactions offers you a chance to make better choices. The more you practice EMP, the more time you spend with your King in control. This doesn't mean the King will *always* be in control, but you can dramatically reduce the amount of time you spend in emotional suffering or destructive behavior patterns. I was reminded of this truth again just this morning. Here's the story:

I got hit with a one-two punch. First, last night my friend's Indian restaurant just a mile and a half from my home was vandalized. The vandals left the hate message, "Go Home ISIS," on one of the walls. Being Indian myself, that cut pretty close to the bone. I heard it often in the aftermath of the 9/11 terrorist attack on the World Trade Center and after the London bombings. Once in line at an airport, a little girl asked her mom if I was a terrorist.

Then this morning, I'm in Trader Joe's picking up some groceries. As I went to stand in the COVID social-distance line, an older Caucasian woman cut me off and berated me in poor Spanish. I discerned that she was telling me that she was ahead of me in line. I told her, "I'm not Hispanic." Then she launched into a tirade, "There are too many of *you people* coming here. You don't know the rules of our country."

I immediately recalled the feeling of being a little Indian kid in a predominantly upper-class white Jewish neighborhood where I didn't fit in. For instance, on parents' day at summer camp, I couldn't eat in the Kosher only dining hall because my parents had brought me Indian food from home. And once in elementary school, while standing in line, one of the kids sniffed me and told the rest I smelled like curry. I was humiliated. I felt like an outcast. I just wanted to be white like everyone else.

Today, standing in line at Trader Joe's forty years later, this lady's words cut through all my years of King's work and stabbed the Kid in the heart.

What was different, this time, was the intensity and duration of my emotional reaction. First, I didn't tear into the woman with a fusillade of anger and profanity. I was able to just say, "Wow, really?" And, at that moment, two different people came to my defense. One was a Hispanic woman. She chastised the older woman and said, "Be nice!" Another gentleman accosted the woman outside the store and told her she was out of line. Second, the intensity and duration that I experienced these emotions were significantly reduced.

In the past, I wouldn't have been able to work for the rest of the day. I would have made sure everyone in my circle knew the story and rolled around in the victimization of some old lady's words. I would have expressed my outrage, and justifiably and righteously stood on my soapbox of a world divided . . . and on and on I would go for days, weeks, and even months. I would add it to the evidence bag of "I don't belong." My kid now had more ammunition to justify an emotional reaction the next time it came!

Now, because of my years of practice, the trigger didn't have as tight a grip on me. I was able to give the King control. I was able to reflect on the fact that not one but two people came to my defense. Instead of living in a community where I didn't belong, I lived in a beautiful Santa Fe community that stood up for others. Not only that, but I just saw on GoFundMe.com that my community raised $50,000 for the owner of the Indian restaurant to rebuild.

Remember, emotional mastery goes beyond looking at the glass half full or half empty. It is about developing a compassionate understanding of how and why we go to the places we go and seeing the impact it has on our lives. When we see how much it costs us, it opens the door to see another reality, a reality that allows us a more enjoyable and richer experience.

## PRACTICE—EMP QUESTION 2:
### What did I conclude?

Revisit the situation you identified in the last practice exercise.

1. Now that you've stripped what happened down to just the facts, ask, "What was my interpretation of the experience?" Be as detailed as you would like to be:

_____

_____

_____

2. Have some fun with this and ask yourself, "What else could I have concluded about that event?" Here's an example that picks on Little League parents to get you into the right frame of mind. One team wins, and one team loses the Little League World Series. Let's look into the minds of the losing team's parents:

   *"We need to practice harder."*

   *"We need a new coach—he's an incompetent moron."*

   *"My kid wasn't played in the right position."*

   *"If they would have put my kid in the game, we would have won!"*

*"I need to take my kid to a better team, it's the lousy team's fault we keep losing."*

*"The other side cheated!"*

*"The referees were making awful calls that gave the other side the win!"*

And on and on and on, opinion after opinion gets expressed. This is actually good news. It means that the conclusions you have reached about the events in your life that give you the bad feelings can be changed. So, now it's your turn. How else could you have interpreted the situation? Come up with at least ten different options. They can be as fun and as outlandish as you can imagine.

1. _____

2. _____

3. _____

4. _____

5. _____

6. _____

7. _____

8. _____

9. _____

10. _____

Some of the conclusions you created are silly, some are serious, some make you feel worse, and some empower you. And . . . you are in control of all of them. The King gets to determine what conclusions serve your life best. When the King is clear about his outcomes, he will create and interpret his experiences in a way that are consistent with achieving those outcomes, which offers you a more fulfilled and richer life.

You are not a victim of this built-in mechanism. As Krishnamurti says, once you realize that you're conditioned, you are now aware of one of your most significant levers for reigniting and reengaging with your life. Here's the bottom line: How you interpret your experiences dramatically impacts the quality and fulfillment and satisfaction you get from life. This is where the rubber meets the road.

CHAPTER 9

# Dancing with Discomfort

You've been lied to . . . The entire personal development industry is selling a myth. It's the myth that you can exist in a state of perpetual bliss and happiness. But it's worse than that. This myth also implies that if you're not experiencing joy and bliss, there is something wrong with you and you need to be fixed. You're told that if you can just take the next course or seminar or program, you'll finally be free from negative emotions. My clients have tried everything: breakthrough weekend retreats, medicinal plants, silent retreats, changes in diets, cold showers, mindfulness workshops, gratitude journals, and hundreds of other practices. While all of them have provided a meaningful experience, the implicit promise of the Kid falling asleep and never waking up again is never attained.

Let's be honest, it's not just the personal development industry pushing this lie. Last year U.S. companies spent over 250 billion dollars trying to convince you that their cars and boats and houses and clothes and colognes and electronics and experiences could give you the joy you've been craving. Why do the personal development and advertising industries do this? Because you and I and everyone else desperately want to believe the lie. The problem is inside us—and we are trying to fix it with stuff outside us.

What is even more insidious than false promises are the false expectations this sets up for us. We expect that, at some point in life, we will have it all together. We hope that we'll live a more satisfying and joyful life because we joined that weekend retreat. We expect that we will now be perpetually satisfied because we purchased that new car or dream home with a view or married a dream spouse. And what happens when these hopes and expectations end up being false? Do we blame the seminars and gurus and material possessions? Nope. We blame and criticize ourselves.

## "WHAT'S WRONG WITH ME?"

The number-one question clients ask me is this: "What's wrong with me?" My high-achieving clients have wealth and material possessions and influential positions in companies, and some are national and international dignitaries. They have all the stuff and achievements the rest of the people are trying to get. Yet, when they get hit with the inevitable triggers and frustrations and anger and negative emotions, they ask, "What's wrong with me? I've done all the work. I've climbed the ladder and rung the bell. I've done everything everyone told me I need to do to feel happy and successful and fulfilled—but I don't!"

If you've ever felt like this, here's precisely what's wrong with you: You are human. You have been hardwired to feel strong negative emotions. Historically, those potent triggers and intense emotions kept your ancestors alive. Today (especially when the Kid hijacks the process), they are focused on your emotional survivability.

> **You are human. You have been hardwired to feel strong negative emotions.**

The third question in the Emotional Mastery Process is "Based on my conclusion, what was my emotional state?" What do we do

when the answer is "Bad, angry, frustrated, betrayed, like a failure?"
We certainly don't want to keep feeling bad, angry, hurt, meaningless,
or like a successful loser. Before we get to that answer, let me share
some common uncomfortable emotional patterns I've seen occur time
and again with my clients.

## Suffering

A common pattern I see in my clients is suffering. We have a struggle or discomfort. We say, "Oh, I'm so uncomfortable," and then we
suffer. We report to friends, "Oh my God, this thing just happened."
We like to get consumed by the story of it all. It gives us meaning.
In *Notes from the Underground*, Fyodor Dostoevsky mocks the plea-
sure to be found in the suffering of a toothache. The Kid learned
very early that if he felt discomfort, all he had to do was cry and
he would be comforted. We were all conditioned to be comfort
junkies in this way. Cry—get comforted. You've no doubt seen a
friend "bleeding" on Facebook or Instagram or at the dinner party
(or maybe you've done this yourself). The Kid is trying to collect
comfort and support, as we've all been taught to do when we are in
the midst of suffering.

## Shame and Guilt

Another typical pattern is shame and guilt. As discussed earlier, this
pattern begins in our development as early as age five. Here's how it
plays out: I meet this problem. I feel uncomfortable with it. I reach
a point of pain. Pain allows me to take action. The presumption is
that I can ask for help and solve this problem. I dutifully follow the
instructions of parents and society and gurus. I have a breakthrough.
But then I find myself in the same spot again, revisiting the same

issue. "Why am I struggling with this same issue again and again?" or "Oh God, here I am again. I thought I handled this. I'm back here again."

Now we begin judging ourselves for having those feelings or taking those actions or not taking those actions. "I shouldn't be feeling this!" It's the double whammy. "Not only do I feel horrible but now I feel bad about feeling bad!" It's an emotional death spiral.

There's a belief that "I shouldn't feel this way, so why am I still feeling this way?" There's a lot of shame around those feelings. "I'm having bad thoughts. Now I'm going to hell," or "My karma is going to be jacked up," or "I'm not grown up yet; I need to be a man (or woman)!" or "Suck it up! Don't show weakness."

These seekers and searchers are very sincere. They are good people. They want to conquer this thing once and for all. Yet, for all their struggle and efforts at destroying it, it returns again.

## Imposter Syndrome

Feeling like an imposter comes from good, sincere people wondering why it is that "I started a diet and got healthy, or I took a course on time management, or I worked on my anger, or I got my drinking under control. So, why am I packing on weight, procrastinating, yelling at my kids, and drinking again?" Clients often ask me, "How is it that I'm a smart, high-achieving rock star who can kick ass and take names and deliver results, but I can't seem to lose ten pounds or control my porn addiction or stop procrastinating?"

There is something in their life they just can't seem to conquer in the long term. They find themselves in an emotional cyclone: problem > success > failure > trying harder > failing again > shame, guilt, and self-loathing. Imposter syndrome may sound like this, "Someone with an achievement résumé like mine shouldn't feel this way. I should feel more successful. So, I'm not as good as other people think I am. I'm not even as good as I think I should be. My inside world doesn't match my LinkedIn profile. I am a fraud." This is classic imposter syndrome thinking.

We present ourselves to the world with the right clothing, cars, and careers. We hide behind the confusion caused by our duality that we don't yet understand. We feel one way about ourselves (unsure), so we present ourselves in another (*everything's fine!*) to conceal the fact that we actually feel inadequate, scared, underprepared, or like a fraud. The Kid is convinced that he is going to be discovered and get in trouble for not being all things to all people, so, you guessed it, we try to be all things to all people. In essence, we double down on our own expired strategies, and "fight or flight" manifests itself right before our adult eyes.

Many successful people have ended up creating pretty solitary existences for themselves this way: judging their own lives by how they inaccurately perceive others' lives, chasing approval and recognition, and their relationships are devoid of any real connection or intimacy. People who you would think have it all often feel a deep sense of loneliness and isolation. In fact, I've been there myself, and that sense of internal incoherence can destroy what most would see as the amazing life they assume you to be living.

Just think about all those in the limelight we've lost to suicide, such as Robin Williams, Anthony Bourdain, and Kate Spade. Many of us spend far too much time perfecting and even doubling down on imposter-driven strategies rather than facing our underlying reasons for feelings of inadequacy in the first place. Often, this obsession with perfection looks admirable to the outside world because it provides a foundation for achieving results and success. But I can tell you from firsthand experience, for those who are caught in the perfectionist trap, it's exhausting and unsustainable, which takes its toll in other areas of life. At the root of this is the warring duality we have within us, which you began exploring in the 5-5 Personality Inventory in chapter 1.

## HOW TO ESCAPE
## THE NEVER-ENDING STRUGGLE

So, how do you escape these suffering-shame-guilt-imposter chain reactions? Before I answer that, let me first share what you shouldn't do. First, don't berate yourself. As we've seen, intense self-criticism is one of the top internal struggles of high achievers. And it does nothing but make the emotions worse. It just adds fuel to the suffering-shame-guilt-imposter fire. This, of course, leads to the second thing you shouldn't do when trying to escape these feelings of self-judgment, shame, and guilt: doubling down.

The number-one fix high-achievers use is to double down on the effort, discipline, self-criticism, and self-punishment. For example, "I need to be even more disciplined, get up earlier, train harder, set even higher goals. I need to do an even stricter diet. I need to promise not to become angry. I need to set up even tougher accountability—and include harsh punishments if I fail." You can do that. And it works—for a while. But this often leads to complete exhaustion from the never-ending struggle. It does *not* lead to a reengaged and reignited life.

The field of CBT/ACT therapy has a brilliant metaphor for this struggle. Imagine you're in a swimming pool with a beach ball. The beach ball represents your negative and unwanted painful emotions. To avoid those emotions, you push them under the water. It's a struggle because the nature of the beach ball is to rise to the surface. But you try to keep an outward all-is-well smile on your face the whole time you're trying to keep that beach ball pushed below the surface.

If you're like me and my clients, you are a master at keeping the beachball submerged. Sooner or later though, you become exhausted or distracted or scratch your nose, and that beach ball bursts through the surface! It is both natural and inevitable that negative emotions will arise. No matter how much you struggle, they will pop up in your face and others' faces sooner or later. As the saying goes, what we resist persists.

So how do we get off the merry-go-round of broken expectations, negative emotions, shame, and guilt and then starting all over again with even more effort and struggle? Let's take a look:

## Have Compassion

First, have compassion for yourself. You are, in fact, a human. You were hardwired to experience the perception-meaning-feeling-action-outcome chain. You can't escape it. It's like being mad at your eye for blinking! Both negative and positive emotions are here for our physical and emotional survival.

At some point in our coaching relationship, a client will express, "It's not fair!" or "Why me?" It's as if they have put themselves in a corner with their arms crossed and are telling me a story with a pouty face. And haven't we all felt that at some point? Let me ask you the same tough question I ask my clients: "Whoever said it was supposed to be any different than this?" Whenever you are upset and your internal voice is saying, "It's not fair!" visualize a little kid in the corner whining and stamping his foot. "It's not fair! This shouldn't be happening!" That is your Kid in his most apparent form.

We've been convinced that we aren't supposed to feel upsetting emotions and so we must do something to fix ourselves. Give yourself a break. Even the world's most powerful and prosperous people feel like you do. All their wealth, power, and achievement haven't erased their human hardwiring and conditioning. My clients are always surprised how much more internal calm comes to them when they stop reacting to their reactions and replace that with simple compassion: "Well, I'm human." And with this calm comes an ability to see reality with more clarity; with greater clarity comes better decisions; and better decisions lead to a better life.

Peace offers us the ability to see more options; stillness gives us the ability to make better decisions. Not only do my clients experience more calm and clarity when they are compassionate with themselves, but they also experience more coherence. Their experience in life begins to match their LinkedIn profiles and résumés. They gain coherence between their feelings and what's actually on paper, and you can too.

## Reset Your Expectations

Second, reset your expectations. None of us will ever reach the place of having it all together in this lifetime. Look at nature. There is day; there is night. A perpetual day would scorch the earth. Consider the tides. The tide flows in; the tide flows out. Without that flow, the ocean's life would stagnate and die. Tune in to your own cycle of breath. You breathe in; you breathe out. We can't perpetually breathe in and in and in. We *must* breathe out. All these cycles and flows exist for our health. There is nothing wrong with you. There is nothing to fix. You are having a human experience. When you expect that you will have highs and lows, you won't be disappointed.

## Celebrate the Gifts

The third step in escaping the cycle of emotional doom is to begin seeing adverse events and emotions as a great gift. Instead of getting angrier, doubling down, and self-flagellating yourself, throw a party. Really, consider the possibility. There is no logical reason you couldn't say, "Holy crap, I'm so uncomfortable right now. I'm going to go buy myself a birthday cake and candles and put a birthday hat on and sing 'Happy Birthday' to myself! I know with certainty that I'm going to have a life-changing breakthrough!"

Here's a fact: The more we transcend our obstacles, the better experience we have in life. The opportunity to have a great experience is rooted in the number of obstacles we can meet head-on, change our relationship with, understand, and put into proper context. This is how we grow and learn. This is how we reach the next levels in our life. Transcending obstacles is the King's way. When we perceive obstacles this way, we can say, "Yes, that was awesome. I wonder when the next opportunity to grow will come?" Remember Ganesh?

By celebrating the opportunity to grow, you transform from the Kid, who reacts to events, has little emotional mastery, and bullies and berates you into an even greater struggle, into the King, who uses the obstacles to reach new levels of significance and fulfillment.

What the most successful people I work with have in common is this: Their relationship with triggers changes from frustration to celebration. They learn to embrace the discussion. And the more you can get awareness and understanding around your triggers, the more you are desensitized to them and the less power they have over you. I call this Emotional ID. As humans, we will all experience intense triggers, but as we work toward emotional mastery, we feel them with less and less intensity and duration (aka ID).

The person who is least triggered wins the game. You end up in a more resourceful, creative, objectively focused place in life. Coaching with me is going through these triggers again and again until you're clear that the Kid is running your life and operating from a place of survival. That Kid is messing with your happiness and fulfillment as a human being without your permission! When you understand the gravity of that, you realize, "Oh, it doesn't have to be as hard as I thought it was. I've been fighting a fight, and there isn't a fight to win. What I'm resisting is persisting. I've had the game wrong." All you have to do is understand that your triggers are your treasure map! That's where the insights and breakthroughs happen.

*The Emotional Mastery Process is a lifelong practice but also has immediate benefits. You are creating a new scorecard in life. Tracking the number of times you're able to anticipate the pattern coming and then choosing differently rewires your brain and keeps your King in the driver's seat.*

This is why I have my clients text me every single time they get triggered. I want them to report in and acknowledge that there is something worth unpacking in this moment of their experience— here lies a treasure. You can continue to struggle and fight against your humanity and your inner Kid. You can go to the next seminar or course or prove yourself with the next achievement. You'll have an expectation that will fix you. But guess what will be there waiting for you? You're going to get dropped to your knees again and again. That's why you're out of fuel.

# PRACTICE—EMP QUESTION 3:
## *Based on my conclusion,*
## *what was my emotional state?*

Revisit the situation you identified in the last two practice exercises. What did you conclude and what were the emotions that came up for you as a result. In the space below, write about your feelings:

_____

_____

_____

_____

_____

If you start feeling your emotional reaction intensify around an event or person, it is a signal pointing to an opportunity to transcend something within you. There is an opportunity in uncomfortable experiences to grow and develop and expand ourselves in a way we were not able to before. We can transcend our triggers and be in a nonreactive place, become a King, and experience more joy. And perhaps, more important, as we learn to have compassion for ourselves, we begin to expand that compassion to others in our personal and professional life. Just as compassion for yourself transforms your inner relationship with yourself, compassion for others causes your most important relationship to deepen, grow, and bloom.

> Just as compassion for yourself transforms your inner relationship with yourself, compassion for others causes your most important relationship to deepen, grow, and bloom.

CHAPTER 10

# Action

In my late twenties, I was a founder of an internet marketing company that was valued near $100 million on paper. I was immersed in the dot-com fantasy of money and prestige and popularity that came with that accomplishment. Then, overnight, I lost it all when the dot-com crash killed the business. I had to lay off employees. I was forced to tell people who had invested hundreds of thousands of dollars in the business, including my father, that their money was gone. I had to give up my lifestyle. I lost relationships. I lost my money. I lost myself and my self-worth. I was deeply in debt. I was a beaten man.

I would love to tell you that I landed on my feet like a jungle cat and rebounded to even greater heights. But the truth is that this devastating personal loss spiraled so far out of control that the conversation in my head turned borderline suicidal. Confronted with failure and embarrassment, I was face-to-face with my deepest insecurities. I became obsessed with the thought that something was wrong with me. It was my inquiry into this question—"What's wrong with me?"—that led to this book. It also led to my being able to help more than 1,500 clients reignite and reengage with their lives.

One of the core discoveries I made initially came from a psychological approach to well-being called neuro-linguistic programming

(NLP), the key elements of which are modeling, action, and reframing. The discovery was this: All those harmful, self-destructive behaviors I had been engaging in were my Kid's attempt to protect me emotionally. How could that be? The Kid would use any behavior it could to protect me from ever experiencing that much personal pain and devastation again. Those behaviors were the Kid's fight-flight-freeze reactions to defend me from perceived threats to my emotional survival. (You can see this in your own life. Look at your five worst traits from chapter 1. How have those traits been serving you?)

But that awareness wasn't enough. How could I stop the self-destructive behaviors followed by shame and guilt? How does one escape the destructive chain reaction? As I've mentioned repeatedly, the key that unlocks you from this cycle of shame and guilt is compassion. You are a human being with hardwired survival instincts controlled by the amygdala. Those fight-flight-freeze instincts allowed your ancestors to survive. And they are still getting triggered daily to keep you alive—even when the trigger isn't a predator. Today, the triggers you and I face are predominantly emotional survivability around our acceptance and approval of others. And everyone does this. Everyone! To protect ourselves, the Kid finds ways to cope. Let's take a look:

## COPING BEHAVIORS AND THE GIFT OF AWARENESS

To survive the trigger-reaction-shame-guilt chain, our inner Kid seeks out coping strategies and discovers addictions. I call these the protective behaviors, and the top offenses I see in this category are easily recognizable actions: overeating, compulsive shopping, drinking, drug use, overwhelm/confusion, overanalyzing (paralysis by analysis), procrastination, compulsive sex, porn, overworking, gambling, gossiping, and sabotaging relationships just when things start to get really good. Moreover, we numb ourselves by bingeing on social media, streaming services, and newsfeeds.

Some of the most successful, respected people you know are silently facing these struggles. So, instead of piling on more shame and guilt for these actions, take a moment to have compassion for yourself and the Kid's instinct to protect. That moment of compassion opens a doorway that can set you free: awareness.

Free of shame and guilt and reactivity, we have a moment to be aware of what the trigger was this time. This awareness leads to understanding. We begin to see patterns in our behaviors (often going all the way back to specific incidents when we were kids). In that moment of awareness, we receive another gift: options. Free of emotional reactivity, the King begins seeing and perceiving new options and possibilities. Instead of being merely passive observers, we see new behaviors that lead to the outcomes we truly desire in our lives. This is where the Emotional Mastery Process becomes transformative.

> **Free of emotional reactivity, the King begins seeing and perceiving new options and possibilities.**

## PRACTICE—EMP QUESTION 4:
### *What action did I take from that emotional state?*

Now that you've identified what you concluded and the feelings your interpretations triggered in you, think about the action you took in that particular instance. There's no need to judge your action. Simply write about the reaction you had in the space provided.

_____

_____

_____

_____

_____

_____

_____

_____

# EXERCISE:
## _Reimagining Your Response to a Triggering Event_

The action you took as a result of that triggering event has already occurred, but looking at it closely provides you with the awareness you need to make changes in the future. This exercise can help you imagine other options you have for responding to other upsetting circumstances and situations. You can use the example you've been working with or think of another event that triggered you—one that caused an over-the-top reaction or behavior you weren't proud of and caused you to self-criticize.

Now ask, "What are ten other ways I could have behaved instead?" Write your answers in the spaces below.

1. _____

2. _____

3. _____

4. _____

5. _____

6. _____

7. _____

8. _____

9. _____

10. _____

## "What Would J.Lo Do?"

If you are having trouble coming up with new behaviors, here's some insight that might help: While in Vietnam years ago, I was approached for a favor by the CEO of the company I was working for. A top music entertainer in Vietnam, who found herself taking actions that weren't serving her, wanted to meet me for some coaching.

I was not sure what to expect as the entertainer didn't speak English and I was going to have to use a translator to have the conversation. She described a very emotional and personal situation that had been really upsetting her. Her description devolved into complaining—and more complaining. It was clear her inner kid was driving her bus. As the complaining continued, I asked if I could pause her story to ask her a question. I asked, "Who is a woman you really admire? Someone you respect, someone who is strong and handles life with ease?"

She said, "J.Lo."

I asked her, "If J.Lo were sitting here right now listening to you, what would she say? How would she handle this situation?"

As the translator asked her my question, I was able to watch her reaction. Her change was instantaneous. I watched her expression as she processed the question. I noticed her posture straighten. I watched her lips curl into a smile, and I saw her Queen emerge. Then she said, "Thank you."

I knew she had gotten what she needed. We've kept in touch over the years, and she mentions often that this simple question helped her put her Queen in charge of her life.

I had another client who would get emotionally caught up in arguments. When asked, "Who do you admire who has the behaviors you would like to have?" his answer was a martial artist he had trained with. As the grappling match would intensify, this martial arts expert would audibly say, "The harder you fight, the smoother I get." My client adopted this phrase as he would find himself getting emotionally out of control in arguments and debates. "The more you argue, the calmer I get." This transformed his relationships with his team and his family.

Identifying with people we admire (whether real or fictitious) is a powerful way to discover new behaviors to replace our patterned trigger reactions. Simply ask what they would do in your situation.

## LOOKING DEEPER

One of my clients was disappointed in himself when he found himself in a road-rage incident. A red Honda had cut him off on the road. Instead of being mildly irritated for a moment, he raged! He chased the car down, rode its bumper, flashed his lights, honked his horn, and pulled up next to the guy screaming and using lots of sign language. After the exchange, he was still raging hours later.

He tried to search the guy's out-of-state license plate. He fantasized about hunting the guy down and doing ninja moves on him. Then, the shame and guilt for his behavior kicked in.

As I worked with him through the 5 EMP Questions, he gained an unexpected awareness. This wasn't the only area in his life that he would rage. He began to see the common thread of feeling disrespected and the subsequent rage that traced back to the feeling of being ignored by his father.

This awareness and knowledge were game-changing. He began to see the trigger coming a mile away. As he saw the trigger coming, he was able to neutralize the reactivity before it ever occurred. He preempted the reactive raging. His King was in control. You can gain the same mastery this client did. You may not be able to recognize the roots of your reactions right away, but by continuing to practice the 5 EMP Questions and doing some self-exploration, you will gain more awareness. Later in the book, you will have an opportunity to examine these roots more closely.

CHAPTER 11

# Change Your Outcome, Change Your Life

It was to be the adventure of a lifetime: A good college and backcountry ski buddy of mine, James, invited me on an adventure skiing the Haute Route—a legendary hut-to-hut ski trip from Chamonix, France, to Zermatt, Switzerland. It's ten days of skiing on the highline of the Alps and is on the bucket list of every backcountry skier.

As I surveyed the equipment I'd need to pack—the 40 pounds of ice axe, crampons, harnesses, and other technical gear—I became concerned. The guys I would be with were in world-class physical condition. In fact, they had just recently summited the Matterhorn together! My ski skills were as good as, if not better than, theirs, but my conditioning was not. I imagined trying to keep up with those guys mountaineering in the High Alps. I didn't want to be the last guy up the climb, huffing and puffing and drenched in sweat while the others waited at the top for me.

Immediately, I set an objective: I've got to drop 15 pounds! I don't need any extra weight to carry up and over these passes. I started dieting and weighing myself. My life became the scale and what not to eat.

Shortly after beginning my mission, I talked about my physical conditioning objectives with a trainer in Venice Beach. He asked me what I was training for—what my goals and intended outcomes were. He asked *why* losing the weight was important to me. Then he said, "It sounds like you don't need a weight-loss program. What you need is a focus on cardiovascular strength. It will build your efficiency. It will keep you from sweating and getting hypothermia as you scale passes. It will help you keep pace with your team. What are you doing for cardio?"

"Yoga, and some running, but I'm not great at it and don't like it," I replied.

"Buy a heart rate monitor now," he instructed. "And call me when you have it."

I did. Then he said, "Here's what I need you to do . . ." First, he had me find a running route that I would enjoy. I was spending time between Encinitas near San Diego and Venice Beach in LA at the time. I chose the boardwalk at Venice beach early in the morning before anyone else was out. There was a perfect 5K setup from Brooks Avenue to Santa Monica Pier. I could cruise my bike down Abbot Kinney to Brooks Avenue every morning and begin from there. Then he laid out a program of training in a heart-rate zone far below my maximum. And to run three 5Ks a week at this lower heart rate.

I really didn't like running. In the past, I'd gone out and run with people ten years younger than me and, worse, some ten years older! It was miserable and embarrassing—not to mention almost painful. It wasn't the blissful experience you see advertised. But running in the morning along the boardwalk, when it was just me, at this slow pace was easy and enjoyable. In fact, keeping my heart rate in that lower zone was hard. At times, my running was more like walking. In the beginning, I was doing a slow fifteen-minute mile. It was a little embarrassing, honestly. The truth was the Venice boardwalk was lined with harmless homeless people early in the morning, and I had no one to impress. I could have been wearing a pink tutu and been fine. After a month or so running the same route, one morning I was greeted with a cheer: "Go, Rocky, Go!"

I followed my trainer's plan—kept consistent and always stayed in the zone. I never once weighed myself during the four months of this training. But, in the end, I'd gone from a fifteen-minute mile to a nine-minute mile—all while keeping my heart rate low. I dropped twenty-five pounds. And I was in the best shape of my life: lean, efficient, strong. All by working easier!

This magic happened for one reason: My outcome (with the help of a wise guide) shifted from weight loss to cardiovascular strength. That is the power of choosing your outcomes wisely. And it's why the fifth question in the Emotional Mastery Process is "Did that action move me closer to or further away from my intended outcome?" Before we explore the power of this life-changing question, let's take a quick step back and review where we are at.

## QUICK REVIEW

Remember, the Emotional Mastery Process is a game-tape exercise. It lets us take a triggering situation or unwanted emotional experience and slow down the speed of thought to review it, learn from it, and change course moving forward. The 5 EMP Questions are

1. What did I observe? What *really* happened?

2. What did I conclude?

3. Based on my conclusions, what was my emotional state?

4. What action did I take from that emotional state?

And now . . .

5. Did that action move me closer to or further away from my intended outcome?

When my clients answer this fifth question, one of the first things they discover is that they didn't actually have an intended outcome! What they had instead was Kid reactivity. The outcomes of the Kid are not the outcomes of the King. Remember, the Kid's move is to survival reactivity—fight, flight, or freeze. These show up in our lives as defending, protecting, blaming, justifying, explaining, rationalizing, and dominating. The Kid will do anything to protect our emotional survivability, sense of belonging, and feeling of being good enough. Sadly, all those unconscious reactivity outcomes take us further away from the King's outcomes of living a life of significance and meaning.

## PRACTICE—EMP QUESTION 5:
### *Did that action move me closer to or further away from my intended outcome?*

Continuing on with the triggering event you've been working with, answer this question as well as you can in the space provided.

If, like many of my clients, you didn't have a clear intended outcome, that's okay. With that awareness, you can start identifying your desired outcomes. What outcome would you have liked for this particular event?

_____

_____

_____

## THE KID VERSUS THE KING OUTCOMES

Here is some fair warning: The Kid shows up in so many subtle ways that we aren't even aware of it. But with practice, you'll begin to antic-ipate the many ways your Kid sneaks to the front of the bus and takes control of that steering wheel.

Let me tell one on myself: When I began coaching more than twenty-five years ago, I loved helping people lead richer, more mean-ingful lives. I loved helping them reengage with life. I loved helping them heal important relationships. But I loved something else as well. I loved feeling like the smart guy with all the answers. I loved being a hero. This fed my Kid's desire to belong and to be important. I too just wanted to be seen, acknowledged, and loved.

As I matured in my own growth and development as a coach, I've learned to let the King take over and make my clients' outcomes primary. I've learned to help my clients use their own intelligence and intuition to reach their own conclusions, solutions, and outcomes. Ultimately, that outcome shift has created far more impact in my clients' lives.

I often see this Kid versus King competing-outcomes battle in the lives of leaders. The number-one complaint of well-meaning leaders is that their teams can't seem to take action without being told what to do. They say things like "They come to me about every single little decision!" or "Why aren't they finishing the project!" or "Why aren't they taking these obvious actions?"

When I work with them through the Emotional Mastery Process, guess what we discover is at the root of many of these problems? The Kid! Why? Because these high achievers thrive off being the hero, being the smartest, and putting out fires. The Kid's need for belonging and approval is actually training these leader's teams to be dependent on them, stunting the team's initiative. Instead of teaching their teams how to think and act, they teach them to do it the boss's way.

To be blunt, many high achievers who become leaders are changing their team's diapers for them! But the energy they brought to being a high achiever—the drive, the early wake-ups, downing a cup of coffee, jumping in to problem solve, and running hard till 10 p.m.—isn't sustainable. To sustain their fuel, leaders need to adopt the King's objectives: developing their team's talent and creating a culture of independence and teamwork.

The Kid's objectives also show up in romantic partnerships. For example, if I feel the need to be heard, I start talking faster and louder, and before I know it, the Kid gets scared and takes over. It thinks, *If you don't hear me, you'll leave me!* In irony, my Kid's outcome is to be heard, but it just pushes my partner away. Or take a man's wife who is trying to explain a tough emotional situation at work to him. What does he do? Listen? No. Instead of a King's outcome (making his wife feel listened to, supported, and cared for), his Kid's objective is to be a hero problem solver. The evening ends with two frustrated people.

Working through the Emotional Mastery Process shows you just how much your Kid's reactivity is highjacking your life. So, what is the way out of this outcome reactivity? It's learning to recognize the difference between the Kid's outcomes and the King's outcomes.

In addition to being reactive, the Kid's outcomes are often external, material in nature. This would be the classic goal setting: "I want a big house, a boat, and a membership at the golf club." There is nothing morally wrong with those goals, but they tend to only disappoint. These goals are often overcompensating for a much deeper insecurity. They train you to look to outside events, people, and things to make you feel good on the inside. And, ultimately, it's not the external things that give us lives of happiness and significance. I love helping my clients learn to set the King's objectives in situations, such as

+ Having a deeper connection with your spouse rather than trying to prove you were right

+ Having the joy of a team that can act independently of your problem-solving prowess

+ Pursuing goals that bring you joy rather than those that bring you the approval of others

It's a process to learn to think about objectives this way. But it begins with simple questions: Did my actions serve me? Did they serve others? Did they serve the greater good?

## EXERCISE:
### *Outcomes of a Triggering Event*

Think of a moment when your actions in response to a triggering event were driven by anger, frustration, and fear. Now ask, "What outcomes did my Kid's reaction really accomplish?" Think of three and write them in the space below.

1. _____

2. _____

3. _____

Now flip the script: Think about the people in that situation. Think about relationships. Think about your actual wants and desires —your internal objectives of joy and significance. Now ask: "What outcomes would have served others? What outcomes would serve the greater good? What outcomes would feed my soul?" Respond below:

1. _____

_____

2. _____

_____

3. _____

_____

## NEW OUTCOMES

One of the most amazing features of an outcome is its ability to draw in, like a magnet, the people and situations and resources needed to accomplish it. A simple shift in outcomes has the ability to transform your life.

I was once working with a very successful client. When we were sorting through his goals and objectives in the different areas of his life, we came to his physical health. Being a high achiever, he set the goal of running a marathon. I asked him if he currently ran. "A few miles, but not consistently," he said. I challenged him on the aggressive nature of the goal. He was convinced he could do it and would enjoy the challenge.

As we worked together, he created great results in his leadership and in his personal relationships with his wife and kids. He was making amazing performance gains everywhere—except his health.

After talking it over, he decided he may need some accountability. Still, no results.

We tried getting a new motivational playlist, custom-fit running shoes, apps to provide his training structure, etc. No matter what we tried around this objective, he wasn't getting results. Finally, after two months of this, we had a heart-to-heart.

"What's really going on here? Why do you really want to run a marathon? What's your real objective?" I asked.

A long sigh came over the phone, and then he came clean with me: "Every year, we take a summer vacation in my wife's hometown. And every year, we go swimming at the local lake. And every year, her ex-boyfriend is there. He's a great guy. I have no animosity toward him. In fact, our kids all know each other, and we all get along great. But he was captain of the football team, and he is still ripped. Honestly, he's genetically superior. I feel like a complete loser next to him when it's time to take shirts off, enjoy the sun, and go for a swim. I'm a pasty-white guy with a doughboy belly. I try hiding with a towel or running in the water before anyone sees me. Just once in my life, I want to be able to take my shirt off and lay in the sun without being humiliated."

"Why did you choose running a marathon as an objective, then?" I asked.

"I thought that if I could run a marathon, I'd lose the weight and be in good beach shape," he responded.

I worked with him on a new objective to achieve a flat stomach. He took some tests and learned that some of the foods he was eating caused inflammation and belly fat. He stopped running to compete in a marathon and started training at an easier pace to burn fat. That summer, he went to the beach and was able to take off his shirt with confidence—all because he shifted his objectives.

Here's the bottom line: If you're feeling awful or less than satisfied after exchanges with your spouse, parents, kids, or colleagues, you need new outcomes to have a better life. Simply put, learning to shift from the Kid's objectives to the King's outcome is one of the most powerful ways to transform your life. And, in the next chapter, I will share some tools you can use to accelerate this transformation.

CHAPTER 12

# Language: Your Words Matter

Language is a tool the Kid wields to control our actions, which means that the language we use is one of the most powerful indicators of whether the Kid or the King is driving the bus. Tuning in to your language can be the key that frees you from your prison of inner struggle and opens doors of possibilities you've been blinded to. It's a critical key to reengage with a life of satisfaction and fulfillment. What we say is intimately entangled with how we think about ourselves and how we present ourselves to the world. And it's often invisible to us! Language can permit Kid Logic to prevail. It sounds like this:

"I'm busy."

"I'm exhausted."

"I would never be able to . . ."

"I could never . . ."

We often use these phrases on a daily basis as though they are true. They are typically unconscious responses that don't get too much attention from our adult selves. Still, they are locking in the programming of the Kid every time they fly out of our mouth. When we talk in this way, we are saying things as if they are fact. But are they? Let's look at this more deeply now.

# THE FLOW OF THOUGHTS AND LANGUAGE

Think of your automatic response phrases as bad code, adware, or spyware. They are not doing you any good. When you catch yourself giving one of these automatic responses, revisit EMP Question 2 and ask yourself what you concluded.

One of my favorite things to do when working with a client is an intuitive whiteboard (IWB) session. During an IWB session, I intuitively question and follow a client's thought flow around an issue or their future. We explore interesting or emotionally charged ideas and thoughts as they come. As we are doing this, I write their exact language on a whiteboard. This is a valuable tool for making a client's thinking and language explicit.

Once I conducted an IWB session with my client, David, a brilliant, successful internet startup CEO. I asked him questions about his business, why he loved the company, what he liked about his role, and what he thought were the barriers to the company's success. The conference room we occupied was ensconced in a wall-to-wall whiteboard. I took notes on the whiteboard, writing down everything David said, line by line. Little by little, as if in a hypnotic state, David's answers just flowed, and I filled the walls with his words.

After a couple of hours, we took a step back and stared at the text-covered walls. "Well, here's your life," I joked.

While we laughed, I could tell that he was becoming more and more uneasy as he looked around. I do many of these sessions, and I love watching my clients' initial reactions as they read and hear what they've said. Then I guide them to weave together their contradictory goals and values and statements in purposeful juxtaposition—similar to the 5-5 personality inventory you did in chapter 1.

What inevitably happens is that much of what they've said doesn't ring true to them when they hear it. They can hear and see their thoughts and beliefs juxtaposed next to the other ideas and beliefs. Immediately, they realize that something's off-kilter. The words don't line up with the way they feel and who they want to be. It's the positive and negative attributes lists going head-to-head on steroids.

We all get trapped in our language and beliefs—yes, even successful CEOs. But if we can take a step back and see our thinking and language, we immediately understand that many of our thoughts are untrue. Our conditioned language has become so normalized that we don't even realize how little consideration we're putting into the words we use. Yet, those very words can unintentionally define our experience.

I have had many clients tell me that this single exercise was pivotal in our work together. In David's case, he saw the outright contradictions as he reflected on them. He also saw the thoughts and beliefs that didn't seem right. He shook his head. "I know I said all of that, and I know those are my words," he said, "but the crazy thing is that so much of this isn't true. It isn't really that way."

As we untangled the writing together, he realized that the patterns he'd developed to describe nearly everything in his life were riddled with contradiction. We were in a room surrounded—"imprisoned"—by untrue "truths," outdated beliefs, and Kid-logic patterns of thinking. His thoughts and behaviors were no longer working for him, but they were continuing to hold him back.

## Your Turn to Explore

Think of the phrases you use that keep you from experiencing your life at the level you desire. Are you creating a prison with your words? What would you do if you weren't "too old," "too young," "too tired," "not ready," "not the right person for the job," or "too inexperienced"? I love it when I have a client who says, "I've never done that before . . ." as if it were a perfectly good excuse for not trying something new!

We all say things automatically as if they were truths and express our preferences without actually considering the impact our words might be having on our experiences. I like to think of this as "Nothing is anything." Everything we describe with language is an interpretation. Language is simply the mechanism by which we explain how we perceive something. You can have two people in the same room, one who says it's hot and one who says it's cold (think about the air-conditioning or heat in your office). So what's the truth? Is it hot or is it cold? We confuse relative perceptions with reality.

We enter the subjective as soon as we use adverbs and adjectives. By beginning to understand and own this, we start to soften and release some of our rigidity and righteousness. And, by doing that, we create more space for ourselves and others too. (Remember, leaders who develop greater compassion and love for themselves can be more effective leaders in the world.)

Whenever you find yourself feeling like something is out of whack, I encourage you to think of it as your signal that something is not internally coherent. It's just a sign that you're out of alignment. You have resistance somewhere, and your inherent adversarial relationship between your Kid and your King is alive and well. When you feel this way, look within for the source.

Have a conversation with a close friend and listen to what language you use. Or pull out a recorder and talk out an issue in a flow-of-consciousness manner. Put the recording away for a day or two, and then go back to it. You'll be able to listen to yourself and gain clarity into your language's influence on your life.

Depending on where you were born, if you were raised in a big versus small family, how active your family might have been in the community, if you had a lot of family traditions, or if there were certain cultural norms that your family subscribed to, you took on this subjective version of the world based on your personal experience. This conditioned experience became your lens for interpretation of life experiences. Consider if that's how you're still viewing the world today.

## REALLY? NEVER?

I once worked with Tim, an executive at a global investment bank on Wall Street. He was actively exploring a new job opportunity in Santa Monica, California. When we began analyzing the opportunity together, I was struck by the language that he chose to express himself. "I could never move to Santa Monica . . ." he said, as if it were the holy truth. "My wife would never buy it."

"Never?" I asked. "Really? Never?" I asked him to think about that statement for a minute. Like David, Tim's truth was rolling off his tongue so smoothly, but had he really thought about what he was saying? He was boxing himself in with three words I've seen many clients adopt in such situations: "I could never."

Our Kid is afraid of getting it wrong, of making the wrong choice, so we use language like "I could never" or "No way" or "That wouldn't happen" to box us in, keeping us safe and out of trouble. (Don't these sound like phrases a kid would use?)

So I asked Tim to flip the statement and come up with ten reasons why moving to Santa Monica could potentially be the best decision he ever made. He reluctantly tried the exercise and slowly realized that many of the raised objections were not necessarily the truth. The moment he began to think about how he could move, his mental doors opened, and he began to imagine the reality. While he didn't end up moving physically to Santa Monica, he did decide that it was time to quit his current job.

When we looked at what made him happiest, he said, "Working out, beer, and golf." So, we started exploring the types of things each one of those worlds needed. After many napkin notes and numerous brainstorming sessions, he identified a niche in the craft-brewing world and an opportunity in the secondary golf ball market. Both strategies were based on consolidation and economies of scale. Within six months of having the inspiration, he applied his analytical thinking skills to solve both needs.

Today, Tim enjoys the satisfaction of knowing he is making a difference in the world. He is hiring veterans and disabled people in the golf business. And, in the brewing business, he is providing a much-needed service to smaller craft-brewing entrepreneurs.

What you think matters and what you say matters. As Henry Ford said, "Whether you think you can or think you can't, you're right." In the next chapter, I will share with you a powerful way to gain new perspectives on your thinking. You'll learn how to slow down your thinking and become the observer of your own thoughts.

# CHAPTER 13

# The Speed of Thought

The 5 EMP Questions are powerful tools to change the quality of your life. They let you see, often for the first time, how the triggers you experience can cascade into decisions that may sometimes not be in your best interest.

As discussed earlier, much of the power of the Emotional Mastery Process is its ability to let you review the game tape in slow motion. Another way to say this is that it puts you in the observer role. You can step out of the fire and observe your thinking and actions in a detached, nonjudgmental way and gain new insights. To help you with this slow-motion replay, I'm going to offer you an Observer Meditation in this chapter. This isn't a spiritual mantra or mindfulness meditation. Its purpose is to teach you to observe your thinking from the perspective of an outside observer. First, let's discuss meditation in general.

## YOUR INNER DIALOGUE
## AND THE ROLE OF MEDITATION

Just as our spoken words are expressions of our beliefs and help define our identity, so do the internal conversations we have in our heads. While we work on changing the relationship we have with ourselves, it is also essential to examine our relationship with the other constant companion in our lives: our thoughts.

Throughout this book, I've emphasized the importance of becoming an avid observer of our thoughts, feelings, and behaviors. The more we observe ourselves in action rather than simply react on autopilot, the more power we have in making a conscious decision to live with the King in the driver's seat. It's really that simple. Meditation is a powerful tool to help you accomplish this.

When I first began the Kid and the King journey, I already had an established meditation practice. I tried many techniques over the years and listened to a variety of teachers. Ultimately, what I found most useful was a meditation that served as an act of observing my thoughts rather than being the one thinking them.

With this form of meditation, you're getting out of your own head. It is the acknowledgment that you are more than the thinker of your thoughts; you are also the observer of those thoughts.

In my years of study and with the help of meditation, I realized that the voice I heard and the thoughts in my head did not have to define me. The voice simply gave awareness to my thoughts that were passing through my mind. Although I was the thinker in actuality, I found that with some patience—a lot of patience at first—I could also be a nonjudgmental observer. I didn't need to believe everything I thought. In fact, a King's favorite comment when observing the thoughts as they come and go is "Hmm, that's interesting." For the King, there's no judgment, no action, and no decision that needs to be taken. He knows that a thought is only what we make of it.

Have you ever had a song stuck in your head? When one of my early meditation teachers asked me to think about this concept, it took me down a profound rabbit hole. It introduced me to another way to look at my ideas around duality and identity—the Kid and the King. To figure out where a song was coming from in my head, I had to consider that there must be two parts of my essence: both the singer and the listener. The moment you are aware that you are both the doer and the observer, you gain freedom. With this freedom, we no longer have to live life on autopilot. We can practice a new relationship with ourselves because we now have a window into our psyche that wasn't there before.

## Removing the Meaning

Many people believe they can't meditate because they think meditation means completely quieting the mind. However, you will most likely always have thoughts in meditation—many of them. The key is to put awareness on the fact that they are just thoughts and to let them float on by as you observe them.

When you detach from your thoughts by becoming an observer, they lose their power. Everything becomes diffused. Anger, frustration, resentment, and judgment no longer exist. You become free to create your experiences as you would like them to be, not as your emotions deem they must be.

Through this meditation, I could detach from my thoughts by watching them as though they were bubbles in a champagne glass, rising to the top, and popping into nothingness. They were natural and harmless when merely observed without my interpretation or judgment. The incessant chatter in my head could come and go without my assigning any meaning to it. Nothing was anything. Just like John Nash, I learned to observe the voice of the Kid in my head.

This meditation gives you an access point to creating a new relationship with yourself. The whole point is to understand that you can be an observer of your life and that you don't always have to be in reaction mode. Further, it offers you the chance to observe the constant chatter in your head without judgment. The moment you can stop criticizing yourself and consequently others is the moment you become free.

## "A Diet of the Mind"

Don't get me wrong; meditation wasn't always easy for me. The process of observing the mind chatter often proved frustrating. Ironically, in my search for a quiet mind, I spent a lot of time trying to get there by fighting with myself. What was most interesting to me about my early experiences with meditation is that not one of my teachers was interested in what the voice was saying or why. They were so deeply committed to their practice and the concept of enlightenment that it was not relevant to them. As for me, I had already gone too far down the rabbit hole to not be asking, "What and why?" I didn't begin a meditation practice to spend the rest of my life in an ashram. I was looking for a practical tool that would help me and allow me to find a reprieve from the seemingly exhausting chatter in my head.

What I found worked best for me was to think of meditation as going on a diet of the mind, just like John Nash did in *A Beautiful Mind*. Would I occasionally go off my diet, mess up, and let my chatter get the best of me? Yep. But I could get back on the wagon when I caught myself, much like I would have after too many tortilla chips and guacamole.

Going on a diet of the mind produced much more immediate and tangible results for my clients and me. Remember, a diet of the mind is about becoming an observer; you are not trying to get rid of the voices. What you're essentially saying is "I am not my thoughts, and I no longer have to be of service to the chatter in my brain or act out in ways that are not reflective of who I am."

## EXERCISE: *The Observer Meditation*

The Observer Meditation is a great way to observe the duality within you. It helps you to understand that you are not your thoughts but a nonjudgmental observer of those thoughts.

You can do this meditation wherever you are.

1. Just for a moment, close your eyes and focus on your breath.

2. Breathe in and out, and keep focusing on your breath.

3. When you feel your mind beginning to wander, bring your attention back to your breath.

4. Separate yourself from what's happening in your brain by observing your thoughts as they come and go.

5. Once you become aware that you are the observer and not your thoughts, continue this process for a few moments.

## SOME PRACTICAL ADVICE

Some people like to begin their day with a fifteen-minute meditation. If you are trying meditation for the first time, start with a minimal amount of time that you can sit comfortably and focus on your breath, even for just a minute. Then, as you progress, extend the time to five minutes, ten minutes, or twenty minutes. The more you can find the time to meditate, the more at peace you will be with yourself.

I personally enjoy meditating for twenty-four minutes daily (a minute for each hour of the day). Over my twenty-five-year meditation journey, I have gone from the extremes (days-long meditation) to simple ten-minute meditations in my living room. When I first started out, I committed to my teacher that I would sit for ten minutes every morning. I failed miserably. I would meditate for one day, skip five days, go back to class, and repeat the cycle. And, when I first began to practice the Observer Meditation, I committed to doing it five minutes a day. Surprisingly, I found it difficult. I wasn't alone; the majority of the other students were also struggling. Why? It was only five minutes!

The teacher suggested that the discomfort of sitting alone with ourselves for even just five minutes was being caused by the judgment we were likely heaping on ourselves. From that moment on, I knew the work that was in front of me: finding a more compassionate view of myself, my life, and others. I had to change my relationship with myself. As you develop a comfort level with your inner self, the deeper and longer you will be able to go into your meditation practice.

Meditation has to fit into your lifestyle for it to become a sustainable practice. There is no perfect way. Think about what makes you feel connected. I like meditating in nature because it allows me to engage my senses and go beyond myself to see the greater picture. For me, this might mean watching the sunrise or sunset from the rooftop deck of my Santa Fe home or skiing the backcountry of Colorado or feeling the ocean's salt spray as I walk along the beach or sitting beneath the stars and connecting with the universe. However, you can make yourself comfortable in your environment, close your eyes for a bit, and breathe slowly and deeply, in and out. It's *really* that simple, and I promise you'll start feeling the benefits after your very first practice.

This Observer Meditation is reflective of the new relationship you are creating with yourself. As you learn to detach and stop fighting with yourself in meditation, you no longer keep fighting with your Kid nor allowing the adversarial relationship between the Kid and the King to continue.

CHAPTER 14

# Looking Back
# to Leap Forward

In August 1914, the greatest shortcut in the history of humankind was created: the Panama Canal. Until that moment, sailors faced life-threatening wind, waves, and icebergs sailing from the Pacific Ocean to the Atlantic Ocean through Cape Horn. As far back as 1513, explorers wished for a way across the Isthmus of Panama. They just didn't have the technology to do it. The Panama Canal slashes three weeks off a modern ship's journey from one ocean to the next. For the ancients, it would have been months.

When my clients use the Emotional Mastery Process to address their triggers one by one through the 5 EMP Questions, they eventually ask me, "Shasheen, isn't there a shortcut to reach emotional mastery even faster?" I'll tell you what I tell them: in a word, yes.

If you've been doing the EMP work, you've no doubt started to see that many of your triggers have roots that reach into the past—often early childhood and teen years. I have two tools to share with you that can help you clear out the roots of these triggers quickly. They are the Kid Letter (which you'll write in this chapter) and the Parent Letter (which you'll write in chapter 15). These are proven methods. The clients I lead through these exercises have made the most definitive and quickest jumps forward on their journeys.

I assembled the EMP tools after discovering that, at the root, many of my triggers were all variations on a few repeating stories and themes. In fact, one of my mentors told me, *"Shasheen, you're just not that interesting."* He pointed out that many of my triggers were all rooted in the same few stories from my past over and over and over.

These letters quickly get to the root of these triggers, but they require some courage. Early in my coaching practice, I would let my clients choose whether they wanted to go there in our work. But, sooner or later, they would get tired of dealing with triggers one by one and just want to get free to pursue their futures. So, now, once my clients have a firm grounding in the 5 EMP Questions, I guide them to take the courageous step of doing these exercises.

> **I assembled the EMP tools after discovering that, at the root, many of my triggers were all variations on a few repeating stories and themes.**

These letters need to be written out and processed—not just thought through. The awareness these exercises provide helps you start making better decisions and choices in your life. More important, the Kid Letter is the best way to develop a new relationship with yourself. It's the most loving, kind, and compassionate step you can do for yourself individually. The freedom and peace that come from releasing the inner struggle is transformative.

The Parent Letter, which follows in the next chapter, is the most compassionate thing you can do externally for others. It gives you an understanding of—and compassion for—others that you have never had access to. The moment you can release any residual stuff with yourself and your parents sets you free. Let's get started . . .

## THE KID'S POINT OF VIEW

As a child who experienced differentness daily and the resulting rejection of my peers, I spent my childhood often feeling isolated and confused. Those feelings never really went away; they just showed up in different ways in my adult life. These patterns of behavior simply wore adult-sized costumes.

Our early fears, wants, and desires, as well as our past neglect, abuse, or a lack of love, didn't just go quietly into the night because we added some sand to the bottoms of our hourglasses. Our inner Kids are still yearning for the approval they wanted as children, even though we are now technically categorized as adults.

While most of us can recall painful moments in our childhood, our canned responses in conversation are "That was a long time ago," or "It's all good," or my personal favorite, "I'm fine." As adults, we rarely, if ever, examine the patterns of those past events and notice the direct connection they have in our adult experiences. These repressed feelings then serve as kindling for triggers in our lives as adults. When our Kid's feelings aren't reconciled, it drives the wedge even deeper between our two personas, and the war between the Kid and the King is intensified.

**Through the Emotional Mastery Process, you acknowledge the Kid's experience as significant and real. If you can accept the Kid's perspective, you can understand why the Kid shows up in your life the childish way he does. You can learn to anticipate the reactions the Kid has to specific challenges, changes, or circumstances in your adult Life. Perhaps for the first time, you will be acknowledged and give voice to that period of your life when you were voiceless, vulnerable, and disregarded.**

## EXERCISE: *The Kid Letter*

In this exercise, you will be writing a letter to your Kid from your King's perspective, allowing you to separate the negative, disempowering aspects of yourself from the more powerful version of you. Read through these directions and suggestions in their entirety and get a feel for what's involved before starting. Then give yourself the time to sit and write. There is no way to do this exercise wrong, but I have noticed that clients who are the most thorough add the most color and examples, and experience the greatest transformation. It doesn't matter if you write or type this letter out. The important thing is to do it, not think it.

---

*Remember, if you are a woman, replace the word* **King** *with* **Queen** *when you write your letter. Again,* **King** *is used for simplicity.*

---

In the letter, the King will acknowledge every painful and disempowering memory in your adult consciousness as it was experienced by your Kid. Resist the tendency to mitigate the experiences of your childhood. Err on the side of embellishment. The point here is NOT to nail the details of your childhood experiences with perfect accuracy but rather to record how you experienced them as a child.

I am not one to dwell on the past, but for this exercise, it is critical to give yourself the freedom to re-create the experience you had when you were a kid. If you have photos of yourself as a child, spend time looking at them and connecting with the Kid inside you before you begin. Enjoy the positive memories too. Take time to reflect on the joy you may have experienced. Then, for the purpose of this exercise, revisit the not-so-great times.

Remember, instinctively, you will not want to go there. Your brain will want to resist recalling those moments of pain and may try to avoid doing this exercise altogether. Push past the resistance and go there. The goal here is to go back in time as an adult today and connect with that Kid inside you. Try to understand the Kid's emotions, feelings, and reactions. Try to be that child and remember what happened, how it felt, and what response you had. The more you can connect with the emotion, the better. Trust me when I say that this exercise is the most loving thing you can do for yourself.

Before writing the letter, name your little you. Naming the Kid inside will automatically create a separation between your two personas. This could be a nickname or just some way you think about yourself. Keep the name association positive or at least neutral. You do not want a name that has a negative association. If nothing comes to you, just put the word *Little* in front of your name and keep it playful.

When I did this exercise myself, I named my Kid Bobby. Bobby was short for Robert Shaw, the American name I had given myself at a point in my career when I was in telephone sales. Instead of Bobby, I could have easily used Little Shasheen or Little Shashi. Remember, the key to this exercise is to establish a new, loving relationship with your Kid. For example, when I did this, I visualized Bobby as ten years old. I gave him permission to be, think, and act like a kid. This helped me remember that Bobby did not have the mental, emotional, or intellectual capacity to process all the past painful events:

+ He did not have the insight to see his parents' actions as loving.

+ He wasn't able to process why he was different from the rest of the kids.

+ He didn't understand the concept of peer pressure influencing his best friend to turn on him.

+ He didn't fully understand how unkind children could be at times or that it might not have anything to do with him.

+ He didn't realize that the other kids were just as confused as he was.

I invited my Kid to say what he needed to say and feel. I listened to him with compassion. I recognized his experience as real.

I've had clients say to me, "Shasheen, can't you just get rid of this Kid?" And this is not uncommon. The sheer omnipresence of the Kid can feel overwhelming. Wanting to get rid of your Kid is normal. But getting rid of the Kid takes us away from compassion and back into an internal struggle. It denies the reality that the Kid will always be with us—and the freedom that understanding brings. As you write this letter to your Kid, your words must come from a loving and compassionate place. Understand that you are speaking directly to the fearful Kid as he works through each memory. This is not always easy stuff for a child to reexperience. (Don't hesitate to speak with a therapist if you find this exercise especially difficult.)

In this first part of the letter, the King will acknowledge the challenging experiences the Kid went through. Be as specific as you can. In the second half of the letter, you will let the Kid know how truly powerful and resourceful the King has become. It is crucial to reassure the Kid that as long as the King is in charge and driving your life only good things can happen. (Use the two-part template at the end of the chapter to fill in the sections with your stories and accomplishments.)

### Kid Letter: Part 1—Recollections

The point here is that even if you only think it happened, write it as if it did happen because it is affecting you. Here are a few tips that will help:

+ Recount as many stories as possible. In fact, go back to the first chapter of this book and review your five positive traits. Do you have a sense that you developed that characteristic because it was the opposite of what you experienced?

+ Use the template for each memory. You want to capture the most emotional and dramatic version of each event possible.

+ Use colorful, emotional words. Capture the experience of the Kid, not of the adult you.

Remember when there were monsters under the bed? It was a matter of life and death in the mind of the Kid. The King must acknowledge the emotional experience here, where the Kid's psyche was at that moment in time. The goal you are going for in this exercise is a compassionate understanding of your Kid. If you can see and acknowledge these memories of the Kid, it will help you understand how this identity was created and why this identity continues to operate from a perspective of fear.

Things happened when you were younger. They were experienced by a version of you that did not have the emotional, mental, or intellectual capacity to process them. Give a full passionate voice to them through the Kid.

### Kid Letter: Part 2—The Gift of Acknowledgment

The intended outcome here is for the King to reassure the scared, hurt, frustrated Kid and demonstrate that everything works out the way it should when the King is driving. Here, you can give yourself the gift of acknowledgment. You are going to acknowledge the King's accomplishments and achievements.

Be on the lookout for the Kid's voice trying to downplay the accomplishments of your life. Even if there are areas of your life that are not optimal or situations that haven't worked out, focus on the positive. If you feel a little resistance, it's okay. When I was initially working through these exercises, I had to reread my résumé and my bio and really think about my accomplishments before giving myself credit. This acknowledgment section is crucial. It sets the stage for a loving, lifelong relationship with the Kid.

Okay, now it's time to craft your letter to the Kid! If you need additional support, visit **www.Shasheen.com/emotionalmasteryprocess**, where you will find some helpful videos and examples.

## The Kid Letter Template

Date:

**Salutation:**

Dear *(little you; name the Kid inside you)*,

**Part 1: Recollections**

*Begin your first section with the statement:*

Thank you for being there for all these years. I can remember how *(terrified, hurt, confused, embarrassed, ashamed, etc.)* you felt when . . . *(Write all meaningful incidents you remember from that time.)*

*Conclude this section with this vital sentence:*

*(Little you)*, I want you to know that the King is here, and I'm going to be driving from now on.

**Part 2: The Gift of Acknowledgment**

*Open your second section with the statement:*

Just so you know, *(little you)*, amazing things are possible when the King is driving. As the King, I can *(fill in the blank)* and I can even *(fill in the blank)*.

*Finish this section with the following sentences:*

*(Little you)*, I just wanted to let you know that I am not kicking you off the bus. I love you, and you're coming with me. However, because of where we are going, I'm going to have to drive from now on. I've got this, and I'm so excited to show you all the incredible places we get to go!

I understand your fears because I was young once too. I want to remind you we've already accomplished quite a lot together and overcome so much, and now we get to do so much more. We're both in for an exciting trip ahead. I can't wait to go on this remarkable lifelong adventure with you!

**Complimentary close:**

Love,

**Signature:**

The King *(YOU! Insert your name)*

Congratulations on completing your letter! Be proud of yourself. I know how much resistance you most likely fended off while going through this exercise. Your skeptical Kid was most likely calling bullshit around the entire process and whispering all the reasons why doing this isn't worth your time. I promise you that it is, and I know your King self recognizes that too. Great job!

Once you've written this letter, sit with it for twenty-four hours and take a look again. Did any other memories come up? You'll know when you've written enough and can simply file it away. Some clients have asked if they should burn it, and the answer is no. This letter is about integration, compassion, and love. Keep the letter around and periodically reread it with the intention of continuing to deepen the relationship between your Kid and your King.

## YOUR KID IS ALWAYS WITH YOU

Remember, the little you—your Kid—will be with you for the rest of your life. And I want you to reread the last part of that statement . . . *the rest of your life*. You are not getting rid of the Kid. Instead, you are acknowledging your Kid as a vital part of you. You are giving your Kid compassion.

When we practice EMP, we learn to recognize when and have compassion for why the Kid shows up in our lives and how to change our relationship to the Kid. Recognizing this is the key to unraveling your suffering. It is the root of the guilt and shame you feel when you behave in ways you don't fully understand. I really want you to understand this, so pay attention:

> *The difference between the ordinary person and someone who has attained emotional mastery is this: Those with mastery have the wisdom to know the conditions under which they can anticipate their kids' arrival and lovingly embrace their little ones before they react.*

You are now gaining the tools to do that too.

At times, your adult self may be frustrated by the Kid's old tendencies and resulting behaviors. But you now realize that it's time to develop compassion for this part of yourself. You learn to anticipate the triggers that prompt the Kid as he shows up in full protective gear. You see the patterns and recognize him *before* he shows up. If he does show up, rather than resist, you learn to simply say, "Thank you, little one, but I've got this." It's time to stop resisting your Kid and learn to embrace it. I promise that you'll feel so much more at peace and exponentially more clearheaded! The choice to live fully as the King is now yours!

CHAPTER 15

# The Parent Trap

Throughout this book, you've seen the impact your Kid's early conditioning has on your everyday life experience—often unconsciously. When I work with clients, I invite them to explore how the most influential relationships in their lives may impact their everyday life experiences. That means having the courage to look at the relationships we had with the people who were most influential during those early childhood years: our parental figures.

Parental figures can include biological, adopted, and surrogate parents—even those who may have left our lives at an early age. They are the people we were most dependent on for our physical and emotional survival. And these are the influential people from whom we inherited both the wanted and unwanted patterns we can observe in our lives today. In fact, you can probably think of one or two of your behaviors that directly correlate with those of your primary caregivers.

The best way I've found to explore these influences is the Parent Letter exercise. In this exercise, you will have an opportunity to unlock a new level of emotional generosity to truly take your game to the next level—because you owe your parents an apology. Did that last statement jolt you? It was meant to. If you had any reaction to that statement, it's because you most likely have some unresolved resentments around your parents. That self-righteousness just bubbled right up to the surface—and that's a good thing for the work we're about to do!

## TURNING OVER THE STONES OF CHILDHOOD

In my experience, people are in one of two places with their parents and their childhood. First, some are clear about their parents' misdeeds: what they did or didn't do for them or to them. Second are those who will tell me that they had a pretty decent childhood and that they have a good relationship with their parents today. I want to address the latter first.

If you are reading this book and have come this far, I know you're not the kind of person who is willing to just settle for your typical ordinary everyday ticktock life. You want more. There is something inside you that longs for a deeper and more meaningful connection to yourself and the people in your life. This is why it is essential to explore the unexamined events from your early life—yes, even the ones you claim to be okay with. We want to turn over each stone to see what might be lurking underneath.

Most people don't see the correlation between the latent anger from childhood and the present-day impact on their adult lives. However, I promise that after this next exercise, you'll be able to clearly see the extent to which it has infiltrated your day-to-day experiences.

Many of my clients tell me, "I'm fine," when I can plainly see they are still triggered by their parents as they describe the current state of affairs. Their Kid is still inextricably bound to them. If you are holding on to even the slightest bit of negativity or withholding love from the most influential people from your childhood, consider that there is an incredible opportunity in front of you right now. Like I said before, this inquiry takes courage, and I know that if you've read this far, you're ready.

Now the flip side of this coin is the belief that you're nothing like your parents. This leads to a life of spending your time proving to everyone that you're better than them and constantly navigating minefields of triggers. Some of my clients have created entire worlds around statements such as "Screw my dad. I'm nothing like him. He was a lazy son of a bitch who did nothing for us." They have structured their lives around not being like a parent (or both parents).

Going one step further, these past events—and your sense of being wronged in them—become the source of your righteousness or your truth as an adult. In fact, I spent much of my adult life feeling like the truth was that I deserved a big fat apology from my dad. I felt my parents needed to acknowledge how they hurt me or I wasn't going to be there emotionally for them.

Some of my clients who had rough childhoods are the highest-performing people I know. Yet, if you're guessing that they often feel unfulfilled or like something is missing, you wouldn't be wrong. However, this type of strategy is exhausting and unsustainable. No matter how good this strategy looks on the outside to others, underneath is exhaustion and loneliness.

> *Our parents, our children, our spouses, and our friends*
> *will continue to press every button we have, until we realize*
> *what it is that we don't want to know about ourselves,*
> *yet. They will point us to our freedom every time.*
> —Byron Katie, *Loving What Is:*
> *Four Questions That Can Change Your Life*

**Important:** This exercise isn't about being good with everything that's happened in your life, and it's not about being fine either. It's about discovering your path to leading life in which you're fully engaged through a thorough examination of any rust you may have on your psyche. Any ounce of past conditioning that is no longer giving you power is ultimately taking away your power. I want to help you clear that path.

With the Kid Letter, you had an opportunity to establish a new relationship with yourself. With the Parent Letter, you have the life-changing opportunity to remove righteousness, disappointment, muted guilt and shame, and to heal your past. But you have to be willing to acknowledge the fact that your conditioning was real and that it is impacting your life today.

## A WARNING . . .

This is one of those inquiries my clients resist. In fact, this entire chapter has a tendency to draw out the Kid's deepest fears and anxieties because we're talking about his parents—the people who were wholly responsible for his mental and physical well-being when the Kid was too young to have a choice in the matter. Here are just a few examples of what your Kid might say (as it elbows you in the ribs) while you're leaning over to turn those stones and bring them into full view:

*"That was a long time ago."*

*"I know my parents didn't mean it."*

*"I'm good now."*

*"I love my mom and dad."*

Another form of Kid resistance to this is the mask of superiority. For example, a successful executive may think they are better than their parents. They have a good relationship with them because they have reached a level of success that allows them to dominate their parents emotionally. It's subtle, arrogant, and harmful.

I can't stress enough how much resistance will come up with this exercise. But the stronger the opposition, the stronger the potential breakthrough you will experience here. You may be coming up with all kinds of legitimate reasons right now as to why you don't need to do this exercise. This is normal. I only ask that you trust me and take this next step, even as your Kid whispers into your ear all the reasons you don't need to do it.

## THE *R* WORD . . .

This process will help you learn to take personal responsibility for everything that has been created in your life thus far *and* enjoy the freedom that comes with that! Consider this:

> *If you are holding on to even the slightest bit of anger, frustration, resentment, negativity, or judgment about your past experience with your parents or other influencers during your formative years, you are ultimately living life as a victim. There is no way around it.*

"I got the short end of the stick," "It's not fair," or "I'm over it" are not statements that form the basis of an engaged and fulfilling life. When you feel the power of letting go of blame, of no longer being a victim, the high-performance version of you emerges. In some ways, I think of this exercise as a selfish one because even though it's a letter to our parents, we're the ones who benefit from it the most.

The healing you will discover as you realize that you've been living as a victim will translate into every aspect of your life. You get to release all the residual anger, resentments, and negative assumptions you have been carrying in favor of love and compassion for the influencers of your early years. In essence, you will become deeply familiar with the true nature of the adult you are and deeply familiar with the

Kid inside you. This will highlight the distinctions that enable you to make choices that allow you to create your life (not react to it) from this point on. You are putting your King in control and allowing your Kid to be a kid.

This exercise is about radical forgiveness and letting the people around you off the hook for how your life is today. It's about becoming someone who is capable of showing up in the world with deep compassion without any expectations of reward. It is also about you taking radical responsibility. To be clear, letting go of the hurt from your past means recognizing that no one owes you anything and that, in the majority of cases, no one ever *intentionally* tried to hurt you. (If you are the victim of child abuse, discuss this exercise with a therapist as needed.)

> **Become someone who is capable of showing up in the world with deep compassion without any expectations of reward.**

Think of it this way: Everyone in your life has been operating from their own past conditioning in the same way you have been. The strategies they've used and choices that they made reflect choices they made from their Kid perspective. If you cannot hold love and compassion in your heart for your Kid, and forgive your parents or others from your past, you will remain a victim to circumstance. If you say, "It shouldn't have been that way!" you remain the victim of your life rather than the hero or heroine, and you will always feel the need to keep that beach ball underneath you. It's just not sustainable if you want to live a life you love.

The Parent Letter continues the courageous self-inquiry and requires a level of honesty about the extent to which your past experience with your parents continues to affect you today as an adult. Anything that you are holding on to from the past, blaming others for, or permitting to make you a victim prevents you from functioning as the King.

*The day the child realizes that all adults are imperfect,*
*he becomes an adolescent; the day he forgives them,*
*he becomes an adult; the day he forgives himself,*
*he becomes wise.*
—ALDEN NOWLAN

# EXERCISE: *The Parent Letter*

In this exercise, you will be writing a letter to a parental figure who was responsible for your upbringing or part of it. Read through these directions and suggestions in their entirety and get a feel for what's involved before starting. Then give yourself the time to sit and write. Like the Kid Letter above, the more thorough, specific, and colorful you can be in your writing, the more you will gain from this exercise. And, again, it doesn't matter if you type it or write it. What matters is that you *do* it instead of just think it through. (Use the template at the end of the chapter to fill in the parts of the letter.)

## *Parent Letter: Part 1—The Rant (Acknowledgment)*

The rationale of the first part is to give voice to the stories and experiences that shaped your life, whether or not you are over them; consider that you're really still pissed off. Express this part of the letter from your Kid's perspective. Go back to when you were a child (from ages four to sixteen) and express the story of what happened as it was experienced by you at that age. Identify as many of these instances as you can. Try to suspend the enlightened version of "I know they were doing the best that they could" or "I am who I am because they were who they were." Dig a little deeper.

If you could go back in time and give them some advice on parenting, what advice would you give them? What's the one thing you wish they knew that they didn't back then? If you have kids, how have you been different? Have you done a better job? How so? What's coming up for you as you read this? Take a moment.

### Parent Letter: Part 2—The Impact (The Courageous Inquiry/ The Admission)

You really want to stretch yourself to identify how any of the residual anger you are holding on to is connected to how you are experiencing your life today. Typically, you will see these patterns appear in your relationships with bosses, spouses, and authority figures, as they tend to show up in the relationships of those closest to you and those with power over you. Ultimately, we feel victimized by these connections and our interactions with them.

Ask yourself what angers or annoys you these days? What kind of people trigger you? What arguments do you find yourself perpetuating? Write out exactly how this is affecting your life and with whom. Here are some thoughts to get you started on this part of the exercise, which you can adapt to your current situation:

*What I realize today is that by continuing to hold on to this perspective, I render myself as a victim, and that is no longer acceptable to me. Anger shows up in how I'm dealing with my spouse/significant other/kids/coworkers, etc. It is fueling my insecurities.*

*As an adult, I'm still trying to prove to the world that I'm good enough and lovable. I still feel like a child when I'm around you, and if I'm honest, I start to regress the moment I pull into your driveway. My inner Kid is still throwing tantrums whenever he feels triggered by . . .*

### *Parent Letter: Part 3—Emotional Generosity*

Share your emotional generosity with your parental figures. Consider that there was never a day that this person or people woke up and said to themselves, "You know what? Today I'm going to totally screw with *(your name here)* and make sure I do or say something to them that they will carry with them their entire lives." Really. Think about it. Do you think they woke up with that intention? The moment my mentor asked me that question, something shifted in me. He said, "Then stop talking and acting as if they did."

Next, imagine what it was like to be them. Understanding, compassion, and acceptance for your caregivers will guide this process. Express your understanding of what they may have experienced as kids and your gratitude for what they gave you, and then (wait for it) let them off the hook. The bottom line is that they had (or still have) parents too. There are generational patterns that are repeating here, and you have the opportunity to now observe and release those patterns.

Dig within yourself for as much emotional generosity as you can harness. (If you just can't find your generosity troves right now, it's okay. Be gentle with yourself, as this can be tough stuff.) The more resistance you have right now, the more the opportunity exists for you to have a life-changing breakthrough as you go through this exercise. Bookmark the feeling inside and consider that taking even the smallest steps toward emotional generosity will have a profound impact on your life. It's a worthwhile journey.

> **Consider that taking even the smallest steps toward emotional generosity will have a profound impact on your life. It's a worthwhile journey.**

What do you know about your parents' childhood? What

experiences did they have growing up that conditioned them? What were their parents like? How were they parented? What was or is their relationship with them like? Where did they grow up? How did they grow up? What was happening in their lives when you were born? How old were they? What was their financial position? What was their relationship like?

Go even deeper. What was it like to have you as a kid? What must it have been like to be parenting you as a child, adolescent, and teenager? What must it be like for them to experience you as an adult? How often do you talk to them? Why? How often do you see them? Why?

If you're a parent today, how would you like to see your relationship with your kids when they grow up? How would you imagine it looks when you're a grandparent or when you're in your seventies and beyond?

There is nothing easy about shining a light in this area of your life. I get it. If you are resisting, just notice the extent to which you can or cannot feel compassion and generosity with your parents as they are today. If you can, what you're going for is something that says, "I am committed to a new and different kind of relationship with you." That may mean spending more time together, calling more often, being less judgmental about their lifestyle and/or choices, or bringing the grandkids by more often. You are merely letting your parents know that you love and appreciate them.

Okay, now it's time to craft your letter to your parents! If you need additional support, visit **www.Shasheen.com/emotionalmastery process**, where you will find some helpful videos and examples.

## The Parent Letter Template

Date:

**Salutation:**

Dear *(Mom and/or Dad; other caregiver),*

**Part 1: The Rant (Acknowledgment):**

*Begin the letter's body with the following prompts:*

I've been really pissed off at you, but I have been pretending that I'm not. *(Insert pissed-off version of your story.)* The truth is, at *(your current age)* years old, I am still holding on to the fact that *(you . . . were or were never . . . you could have . . . you had the audacity to . . . How could you . . . Why the hell did you . . . Why didn't you . . . I can't believe . . . WTF?!)*

**Part 2: The Impact (The Courageous Inquiry/The Admission)**

*Begin the second paragraph with the following prompts:*

By holding on to this perspective, I continue to render myself a victim in my own life and that is no longer okay. The truth is the victimization and latent anger show up just about everywhere in my life. It shows up at home with *(fill in the blank)* and as *(fill in the blank)*. It shows up in my career with *(fill in the blank)* and as *(fill in the blank)*. The truth is it shows up everywhere and I'm ready to let it go. (See how many places you can identify and continue to add to the list.)

The goal here is to connect the dots in a way that you have never connected the dots before. How? The more detail and the more honest and uglier it is, the greater the breakthrough that is available on the other side.

**Part 3: Emotional Generosity**

*Begin this paragraph with:*

What I realize now is there has never been a day when you said to yourself, "Today I'm going to F@! with *(your name)*." I can see now you were doing the best that you could. I can't imagine what it must have been like for you. *(Use the earlier cues to complete the following.)* I know you grew up with . . . I know your mom/dad never . . . I know you never . . .*(Keep going . . . give as much as you possibly can give, and give it freely.)* I want you to know that there are many things that I appreciate about you (fill them in). There are many positive things that are in my life because of you such as (fill them in). I want you to know that today I am now taking 100 percent responsibility for my life and I'm officially letting you off the hook. I want you to know that I'm committed to *(more time, communication, effort to, etc. Dig deep)*.

**Complimentary close:**

I'm sorry. Please forgive me. Thank you. I love you.

**Signature:**

*(Insert your name.)*

Now, what do you do with this letter once you've written it out? I don't recommend you send this to your parent(s). Much of this work was for you. But, if you're comfortable, you can always read it to them in the future if you choose to do so. If you do read it aloud to your parent(s), for the greatest impact, soften your rant and amplify your generosity toward them.

# REFLECTION ON MY PARENT LETTER

The Parent Letter proved to be a liberating process for me, and it helped me find the King version of myself. I had to face my history, conditioning, and experiences to create a new relationship with myself. It took determination and courage to see that through.

I progressed from wanting my parents to disappear to not speaking with them, to agree to disagree, to "I love them, but they are still idiots," to "I'm fine," to my realization at forty-something-years-old that I was still angry and giving them the power to trigger me. Writing this letter allowed me to let my parents off the hook 100 percent for everything that has happened in my life. I was finally free to be responsible for my own experiences.

At first, this was terrifying. I mean, if my parents weren't the villains I had made them out to be, then who was the villain? As it turns out, I was the common denominator in all the unpleasant experiences in my life. Today, my relationship with my parents has transformed. And the decision to continue to move toward emotional generosity, compassion, and love for the two people I had to rely on for my physical and emotional survival as a child has had a profound effect on my life.

The changes we've experienced in our relationship took a lot of work on my part. There was a lot of wasted energy that I was holding on to very tightly. I have found that the more energy I exert toward generosity, compassion, and love, the better my personal experience is when we interact. Releasing them has been one of the most significant changes in my life. We look forward to speaking with one another and spending time together. It is quite different from the past when it was superficial and strained.

I have discovered that anything short of compassion and love for those in your life, or in your past, leaves you with residual feelings that need to be examined. This letter-writing process will help you to see where you still have work to do on your way to becoming your fully empowered King.

You can use this three-part letter structure not only for your parents but for anyone you are holding resentment toward.

## RECONCILIATION & FORGIVENESS: HO'OPONOPONO

I want to give you another tool for your forgiveness toolkit. This one might feel a little strange at first, but it's quick and easy to do, and it creates profound results. It's called the Ho'oponopono, and it works beautifully with anyone in your life toward whom you are holding resentment.

The ultimate goal is to let go of any of your resentments—not just with your parents and caregivers, but with EVERYONE. Yes, I said, everyone.

The Ho'oponopono is a Hawaiian practice of reconciliation and forgiveness. It contains four simple sentences that can be repeated silently or out loud. Although the sentences are simple, its effects are powerful. This mantra is powerful for releasing anger and resentment and giving you an overall sense of calm and great compassion for others.

Think of someone you've been holding resentments or anger toward. Then repeat the following (again, silently or out loud) while thinking of them until you start to feel any negative feelings around that relationship begin to fade:

*I'm sorry.*
*Please forgive me.*
*Thank you.*
*I love you.*

There has been a lot of research about how and why this works, and I encourage you to do a little research yourself if you're skeptical. It's powerful stuff! While your relationship with that person won't necessarily improve magically overnight, you will absolutely start to feel the negative emotions you are holding on to begin to dissipate. I promise you that it has the power to change your perspective and your entire life experience if you let it. If you have any doubt, do yourself a favor and monitor your triggers and run them through the 5 EMP Questions. I can tell you with absolute certainty that the dots will connect, and you will see that which you may not have seen before.

The EMP Process: The 5 questions, the Kid Letter, and the Parent Letter have given you great insight into how the Kid has been driving your bus. Now, in the next chapter, you'll discover how the Kid keeps you inside self-imposed cages.

*Forgiveness is the fragrance the violet sheds*
*on the heel that has crushed it.*
—MARK TWAIN

## CHAPTER 16

# The Edge

*Life begins at the end of your comfort zone.*
—Neale Donald Walsch

Imagine being caged your entire life. Then one day, your cage is opened, and you are set free. Would you run, skip, explore? In the Blue Ridge Mountains of North Georgia, Project Chimp set six male and nine female prisoners free. These prisoners were research chimpanzees who had spent their entire lives in cages. They were released onto a specially designed, six-acre, forested habitat.

In a video of the males being set free, you can see it takes the chimps awhile to embrace their freedom. One by one, the chimps stand at the threshold of freedom, look outside, and then retreat back into the comfort of the cage. Then they come and look out again, look up at the sky, look to the forest, and then go back into the cage. Finally, one chimp, Lance, makes the step to freedom. The others just watch him. He coaxes them out a bit, one by one. Even when out of the cage, they don't move too far away at first.

I observe this same behavior in clients. They have done the EMP work and have taken a deep dive with the Kid Letter and the Parent Letter. Week after week, they have walked through the 5 EMP Questions with me on the endless triggers that life throws at them. They have connected the dots and see the patterns in a way that they have never seen before. They see the disempowering meaning that keeps getting created and re-created time after time. And one day suddenly there is more oxygen in the room; there is a new freedom and facility with the triggers of the past. They stand at the threshold of their comfort zones and see a new world before them . . . and they often retreat back into the comfort of their cages!

My goal in this chapter is to call you out into your new life and future—to coax you past the edge of your comfort zone into a life that reengages and reignites you. And to do that, I need to guide you through a few of the common Kid-logic patterns you'll have to face.

## YOUR GREATEST FEAR

As my clients work through the Emotional Mastery Process, they learn that many of their motivations and drives and even positive personality attributes were just early conditioning and reactive patterns from their childhood. They learn that many of the things and people they blamed their struggles and challenges for weren't out there but were internally generated.

This brings them to the threshold of freedom. They are no longer motivated by proving or pleasing. They are free to pursue what they want just because it brings them joy.

Much of the blaming and victimization patterns are replaced with a King-like focus on outcomes that serve themselves, others, and the world. But as they stand at this threshold of a new life, they become disoriented. Suddenly, the fuel that drove their early success is gone. So are the anger, frustration, self-criticism, and adrenaline-fueled drive. They are free to dream their own dreams, explore new worlds, create new relationships, and experience a level of significance that has evaded them until now. And yet they hesitate . . .

Why? In a word: *responsibility*. The realization hits them that, for the first time in their life, they are free. That means that they, and they alone, are responsible for the results of their efforts. There's no one to blame if things don't work out. No one to point fingers at. Their villains are gone. And in that moment of clarity at the threshold of freedom, who rushes in to save them?

The answer is predictable by now, isn't it? The Kid. Nobody hates being responsible more than the Kid. No one wants to be comfortable more than the Kid. Remember, the Kid's prime directive is to keep us physically and emotionally safe and comfortable. Responsibility is neither safe nor comfortable. Neither are big, bold new dreams, new relationships, or new worlds. So, the Kid rushes in to save us—to pull us back into the comfort zone of the cage.

## SELF-IMPOSED CAGES

We create these self-imposed cages for ourselves on both small and grand levels, in both our personal and professional lives. We put ourselves in figurative cages. And when we feel a door swinging open to let us out, the Kid steps in to make sure we stay right where we are, thereby averting any danger.

We've established that the Kid's worldview is far from boundless. So it follows that he would want to keep us limited (remember, he is protecting us, and his intentions are good). But regardless of the Kid's altruistic intent, this is the pattern that I would bet has been a source of tremendous pain in your life due to missed opportunities and risks you decided were too great to take. Anything that takes us out of these cages carries with it the risk of looking bad or of outright failure. This ties us back to the existential childhood wounds. In Kid logic, this is the pain your Kid will do anything to avoid.

## Everyone Has an Edge

First things first. No matter their level of success or mystique, everyone has an edge to their comfort zone . . . from Warren Buffett to Bill Gates to Sheryl Sandberg. Past accomplishments, career titles, and/or the most expensive education will not let you escape from it. Wherever you are in life has been defined by an edge, no matter what you've done or the level of your accomplishments.

Let's examine this concept of the edge through the parable of the thermostat. Think of your identity as a thermostat in a room. Imagine your personal comfort zone is set to a comfortable 73 degrees. If the thermostat dropped to say 68 degrees, the King would adjust it and turn it back up to the temperature he's used to, a pleasant 73 degrees. Of course, you'd hear no objections from the Kid.

He liked it that way because he was used to it. And there's a delicate balance here. Let's say the temperature drops slowly, little by little like it typically does. We allow one thing into our lives that doesn't belong, and then another, and little by little, we begin to accept this as our new reality. By the time we realize how bad it is, it's too late; we are already frozen.

Now, here's how this plays out in real life: By the time we're in our early to midthirties, we've become pretty set in our ways; we've gotten comfortable with the phrase, "This is just how I do things." This is essentially the set point of our personal thermostat. We're comfortable here. We're in our comfort zone, and this becomes the level at which we're self-regulating. In most cases, on the surface, it looks like the good life.

If anything changes in our lives and pushes us outside this setting in one area or another, we will self-adjust. For instance, our relationship is going great, so we start instigating arguments. We reach our desired weight, so we start eating more food. We get a promotion and a raise, so we start overspending and create money problems for ourselves. We see this money problem all the time with lottery winners and athletes who have more money than most people could dream of but end up deeply in debt. It's because the identity, or the temperature, they've set for themselves is not consistent with their psychological state. Something inside them doesn't believe they are worthy. They've reached a make-believe level that was comfortable and adjusted back to it. In other words, whatever we've achieved, whatever has been responsible for our successes up until now, is, by definition, the very thing holding us back from going to the next level. In the book *The Big Leap: Conquer Your Hidden Fear and Take Life to the Next Level,* Gay Hendricks, one of my mentors, eloquently describes this phenomenon as one's "upper limit."

## The Kid's Edge Brought You Here

The current edges we have in place are how we ended up getting to this moment in time. And as you get closer to getting to your real life's purpose, the Kid's voice will only get louder. This is why the Kid Letter is so important. And again, while being a particular way has gotten us so far, it is important to come to grips with the fact that the Kid's coping strategies expired a long time ago.

We feel much of our discomfort because the way we are coping with it is outdated. We know that the limited version of us is not who we are meant to be today. We know this because we are not experiencing the kind of joy and satisfaction we should be experiencing at this point of our lives. We know this even as we sit in our executive office operating from a six-year-old's life strategy. It's time to let go of our dependence on expired strategies and take steps that will empower and propel us to the next level of life.

# WHAT YOU CAN EXPECT

*Our deepest fear is not that we are inadequate.*
*Our deepest fear is that we are powerful beyond measure.*
—Marianne Williamson

Let's look at some of the common patterns I've seen repeatedly in my own life and the lives of my clients when we reach the edge of our comfort zone. Knowing ahead of time what you can expect your Kid to do when you try to reach beyond the edge helps you navigate past the comfort threshold and into your brave new world.

## Hedging Bets

One of the biggest ways I've seen clients pull back from freedom and responsibility is hedging their bets. This is a pattern I was personally a master of. Here's the story of how I got so good at it.

I vividly remember being ten years old and getting a 99 percent on a test. After school that day, I proudly walked into my father's office to tell him the great news. I strode right in and declared proudly, "Dad, I got a ninety-nine on my test! The highest grade in the class!"

After a momentary pause, he looked up, and with his classically stoic face, he replied, "Well, what did you get wrong?"

Caught like a deer in headlights, the proverbial balloon I was holding quickly drained of air, and I stood there, not immediately knowing how to answer. Finally, I said, "I don't know."

"How are you going to be able to grow if you don't learn from your mistakes?" he asked.

This was a perfectly valid point and a good life lesson, but there was no way I could hear that at the time. Instead, what I heard was

"You're an idiot. You're an embarrassment. How could you be so stupid?"

I wanted to see my dad smile and say, "That's awesome, son!" or "Great job!" or "I'm proud of you!" What I took in at that moment instead was the belief that I would never be good enough until I got 100 percent. My dad's definition of excellence got translated by me at that moment as perfection—it was Kid logic in action. This Kid experience led directly to my beliefs and actions as an adult.

I was never without an excuse for failing again. I'd set up viable, reasonable excuses in advance. I began living my life like a marathon runner who was committed to running but, three months before a race, would find a brick and drop it on his own foot. This would kill the expectation that he could do anything but make it through the competition instead of winning the damn thing.

In today's world, I might even post the fact that a brick had fallen on my foot to Instagram (with a sympathy-inducing photo, of course) where I could receive support for my new predicament in the form of, "Get better soon!" and "Are you going to be okay for the race?"

On race day, I would proceed to grimly run the heat from the back of the pack. Of course, nothing too great would be expected from me as I had just dropped a brick on my foot . . . so there was no risk of failing. I had already set myself—and everyone else—up for the fact that I would do what I said I was going to do (because I'm "a finisher!") but that I wasn't going to be capable of 100 percent.

Although it seems so clear now, it took me a long time to realize that I was the one who was continuing to drop bricks on my own feet. Deep within my psyche lived the story of the kid who got 99 percent on his science test and still wasn't good enough for his father. So if I wasn't ever going to be good enough, I needed to put protective measures in place so that in any area of my life in which there was a chance I might fail, I would have my out.

⨾ 155 ⨽

Whether in my business or other aspects of my career, my romantic life, or my familial relationships, there was a chance that I might not get it right 100 percent of the time, so I hedged my bets. Can you think of some ways in which you might hedge yours currently?

## Procrastination

Procrastination always leaves a door open through which we can make our exit. I am officially the master of procrastination and the mogul of distraction. I invented more ways than you can imagine to avoid writing this book. I was secure in my record of success using the techniques and strategies you've been reading about and was seriously committed to sharing this wisdom to make it accessible to others, but I was still procrastinating.

I had a meaningful purpose, but my resistance showed up. Instead of focusing on writing this book, I put energy into things I knew would have positive outcomes, such as my current clients, my health and wellness, focusing on my home environment, focusing on my outdoor living spaces, and cultivating fabulous friendships on the ski slopes. I wasn't focusing on what I had told myself mattered most.

Think about it this way: *If we actually executed a project the way it was intended, completed the outline, followed the instructions, started thirty days before the deadline, and worked diligently through the process, and it still wasn't good enough, then what?*

Pass or fail, the results are inescapable at that point. This is another facet of the Kid's fear of responsibility and failure: that he still won't be good enough despite his best efforts. But the Kid's deployment of procrastination saves you from experiencing that stark responsibility and its reflection on your worth. This is why procrastination is one of the worst offenders in stunting self-growth.

## Resistance—Exhaustion and Overwhelm

Many of my clients complain about too much to do, too much busyness and exhaustion. These clients are wildly successful but believe that to gain more success, they will have to do more of what is exhausting them. This is an exercise in the Kid's reaction mode. This type of resistance is based on a fundamental belief that you will not be good or perfect enough to do more than what you have managed already. If you feel perpetually tired or overwhelmed, ask yourself if one of your Kid's beliefs is getting triggered. You might be replaying a story in your mind that is no longer helpful. There's a good chance you may be avoiding that big step outside your cage of comfort.

## Resistance—Addiction

> *Most of us do not take these [difficult] situations as*
> *teachings. We automatically hate them. We run*
> *like crazy. We use all kinds of ways to escape—*
> *all addictions stem from this moment when we meet*
> *our edge, and we just can't stand it. We feel we have*
> *to soften it, pad it with something, and we become*
> *addicted to whatever it is that seems to ease the pain.*
> —PEMA CHÖDRÖN

Food, television, work, drugs, alcohol, the gym, sex, or anything you overuse to escape feelings you do not want to feel or avoid actions you do not want to take is an addiction. In my experience, people who use external distractions too much actually become victims of their own avoidance.

What is interesting is the number of times I have seen the

addiction pattern in my clients who can't recognize it because they don't/won't associate themselves with the word *addict*.

We also need to distinguish between the idea of healthy versus unhealthy addictions here. Being addicted to the gym may appear better than being addicted to alcohol. But whenever we feel we have to do something or don't have a choice in the matter, it is problematic. I've seen clients who work out obsessively, and it's totally based on fear—not on the desire for a positive outcome. When you get right down to it, it's punitive in nature. Every single one of us is addicted to something we overuse to make ourselves feel safe. This is a resistance to surrendering to the truest, most powerful version of ourselves.

## Other Ways to Pull Back

Here are several other ways I've observed that our Kid gets us to pull back from our edge:

+ Inability to make decisions

+ Self-sabotage

+ Confusion

+ Frustration

+ Overreaction

+ Oversensitivity

My Kid has used all these and more. It was clear that as long as I occupied any of these static, indecisive places, I didn't have to act. It was the mechanism that allowed me, as well as my clients, to avoid responsibility.

Think of procrastination, confusion, and all the various forms of bet hedging and self-sabotage as simply the mechanisms the Kid uses to keep us from risking failure. After all, as long as we're engaging in self-sabotaging behaviors, we're not out in the world putting ourselves at risk. And even if we try to go for it, we've got a good excuse why it didn't work out (enter brick on foot).

I'm going to assert that the Kid would rather see you hanging out on the couch watching TV, bingeing on Netflix, and playing video games than going out into the scary world and risking discomfort and failure. Think about how all these common behaviors serve us by not letting us move forward and ultimately by letting us avoid taking responsibility for our lives.

## The Flip Side of the Positives

There's a flip side to this Kid's toolkit of bet hedging and self-sabotage. There is a whole other set of tools in the top drawer. I purposely say top drawer, as these are characteristics we adopt that actually look great on the surface. They don't look like drinking too much, overspending, avoidance, procrastination, or being overly critical or argumentative. Still, they are emotional survival strategies that our Kid pulls out all the same.

Go back to the first exercise you did in chapter 1 for a moment and think about the answers you gave to your five best and worst traits. The attributes you listed there—both good and bad—are actually the source of these additional tools. Attributes you listed, such as generosity, kindness, or compassion, are wonderful. Still, they can also be used to mask frustration, avoid conflict, or allow us to stay on everyone's good side.

*If I'm never angry . . .*
*If I do what I'm told . . .*
*If I am everyone's friend . . .*
*If I pick up the slack . . .*
*If I always help out . . .*
*If I never say no . . .*

They are all some form of "I will be a good boy or a good girl and remain safe, acceptable, and lovable." Using these tools from the positive attribute toolkit can remove your personal boundaries with the net effect of letting people walk all over you. Remember, the foundation of your positive attributes was how you were conditioned as a child, and these positive attributes are also the foundation of your edge. Using them will prohibit you from living an outcome-driven life.

Although innately good, these characteristics are acting as a mask when utilized in this way. Easygoing, fun, and gregariousness are all great qualities, but not if they come at the expense of you finally pushing that personal edge.

## HANDLING THE KID'S RESISTANCE TO THE OUTCOME-DRIVEN LIFE

It's important to be aware of these patterns of Kid logic and emotion as you step on the path to a bigger life. Your Kid is going to object. Loudly. But don't worry; this is simply resistance, Kid logic, and the Kid's quest for self-preservation. This resistance will similarly come up whenever you establish new goals, go in new directions, or embark on a new career or other unknown ventures. The Kid doesn't want you to change or fix anything because, ultimately, he would rather stay in the cage he's accustomed to rather than experience the potential discomfort that comes with change. He would rather say, "What are you talking about? Look how far we've come!"

Don't put any focus or meaning on these feelings as they come up, just for right now. Your job at this moment is merely to quietly reassure your Kid that there are no metaphorical monsters in their closet.

Getting to live in your fully outcome-driven life will make you uncomfortable from time to time. Your Kid *will* show up. You can bet on that. I call this dancing with discomfort . . . and it's completely unavoidable and inevitable. You can't stop the waves, but you can learn to surf!

Growth is not always comfortable; there is a reason they call growing pains *growing pains*. Unfortunately, society has been conditioned to believe that something's wrong in our world or wrong with us when we feel discomfort. Instead, I encourage you to explore uncomfortable feelings when they come up. Don't run; don't bury your head in the sand and say that everything's fine. That just puts you in resistance. Your goal is to be in the flow, flirt with the edges of discomfort, lean in, and nurture your personal expansion.

## EXERCISE: *Dance with Discomfort*

When you are faced with an experience that brings you discomfort, dance with the discomfort by doing the following:

1. Witness this dynamic within you as it starts to unfurl.

2. Feel the feelings that come up. Ask yourself, "What's coming up for me in this present moment?"

3. ID the feelings of discomfort. (ID stands for intensity and duration.) Your job is to identify that you're uncomfortable and determine what you want to be the intensity and the duration of the experience. Remember, this is all just part of a pattern that will come up for you and has been coming up for you for many years. There is no shame or guilt here.

4. Acknowledge your Kid's fears. Reassure him that he is safe, that your King has this under control, that great things are on the way! Your King says, "Oh, there you are, little buddy. I see you; I got this. We're good."

5. Ask yourself what you truly want, and take your next steps accordingly.

What I fervently want you to get is that when you learn to identify the discomfort and, in turn, disarm the Kid's fears, you can then reconcile this part of yourself. And when this happens, your edge will move! Once we see our patterns of behavior, the patterns lose their power.

> *What we're talking about is getting to know fear, becoming familiar with fear, looking it right in the eye—not as a way to solve problems, but as a complete undoing of old ways of seeing, hearing, smelling, tasting, and thinking.*
> —Pema Chödrön

## UPGRADE YOUR OPERATING SYSTEM

Since 1985 there have been over thirty releases of the Windows operating system. In each version, Windows created an upgrade to withstand the expansiveness of the programs and functionality that became possible due to the operating system in current use. In each version, users suffered and experienced various levels of discomfort. Yet, Microsoft's developers systematically rectified each challenge with their weekly critical updates, Eventually, these led to the next complete system upgrade.

We are no different; we have to keep expanding. What gets delivered to us in our life experience is just another opportunity to give ourselves an update. The dance with discomfort is nothing more than that. Experience the discomfort and manage the intensity and the duration of that discomfort by examining the past conditioning responsible for the perspective. And I can't stress this enough: *The discomfort will be inevitable, and the triggers will happen. Much like the number of updates your computer will need during its operable lifetime, this will be a lifelong process for you too.*

You've been operating with Kid logic in the background without even realizing it. If you're reading this, you're obviously someone who has achieved some pretty amazing results and are the kind of person who is looking to better themselves. But if you will go any further in realizing those dreams that have long since been tucked away or unlock your crazy amazing potential, it's time to accept that Kid logic has gotten you as far as you can go. It's time to upgrade your operating system from Kid to King.

Step one is getting your feet unglued and kindly, lovingly telling the Kid, "Thank you for trying to protect us, but I've got this now, and I'll take it from here." The edge is calling you. And you will never have the life you desire unless you step over that line in the sand and kick up some dust.

Let me tell you about one of my heroines who courageously stepped beyond the edges that family, society, and culture placed on her. My mom, an educated Indian woman, was ahead of her time. Her parents used to tell her that her eyes would fall out if she kept studying so hard and that her job was to get married and become a good wife. Though she eventually became a successful doctor and pathologist—as well as a good wife and mother—she was cut off by her family because she dared to dream outside the boundaries of a role that was projected onto her. She and my father only had each other. As an Indian-educated, immigrant woman, she recently retired as the director of pathology for one of New York's most prestigious hospitals.

I'm not gonna lie. It's incredibly uncomfortable rubbing up against something as solid as an edge that's been in place for a very long time, especially when you have at least one of your feet being actively nailed in place by your Kid. The Kid's world is all about avoiding responsibility. Yet, as your King self, you know it's finally time to start taking responsibility for your gifts and dancing on the edge. And in the next chapter, I will give you a King's toolkit for living that bigger life.

# CHAPTER 17

# Tools for an Outcome-Driven Life

Congratulations! Because you were willing to take a chance on this journey with me into courageous self-inquiry, you now know how to live more completely as your fully realized King self. I sincerely applaud and honor your efforts and dedication to this process. Now, you can stand confident in the fact that your King—the part of you that knows how to make things happen—has the upper hand. You dared to take an honest and thorough look at your past and current relationship with yourself and turn over the stones that most people will go their whole lives leaving unturned.

## EXPECT PREDICTABLE TANTRUMS

Will your Kid self still throw the occasional tantrum as you move forward? Yes. Drop the odd brick on your foot as you try to run that future marathon? Absolutely. Hedge some bets here and there? You can bet on it. But now, you recognize your Kid's reactions for what they are (loving and well-intentioned!) and know that you don't have to operate from this place any longer.

You have the tools to recognize your triggers, which will still appear as they always have. Yet, now you can call upon the King to elevate your experiences and manage your responses. When you are driving the bus from this mindset, you will have successfully upgraded your operating system.

Your Kid isn't going anywhere, but you now have the depth of understanding to lessen the intensity and duration (ID) of your response to external triggers. You are actively forging a new relationship with yourself; it's not about your job, it's not about losing weight, or resolving your issues with your partner. Now you can claim responsibility for yourself as the source and the creator of your own life.

# EXERCISE:
## *90 Days Living the 5 EMP Questions Challenge*

Rule number one: Don't forget to practice Emotional Mastery Process beginning with these five questions. They hold the key to decreasing the amount of time you spend in nonproductive emotional states. Conversely, they hold the key to living a rich and fulfilled, outcome-driven life.

So, starting now, I challenge you to ask yourself these five questions daily for the next ninety days. Whenever you experience any kind of negativity, pause, breathe, and reflect on these five questions. As my clients can attest, this simple practice will transform your life. Here are the five questions again:

**EMP Question 1:** What did I observe? What *really* happened?

**EMP Question 2:** What did I conclude?

**EMP Question 3:** Based on my conclusion, what was my emotional state?

**EMP Question 4:** What action did I take from that emotional state?

**EMP Question 5:** Did that action move me closer to or further away from my intended outcome?"

When you become a master of these five questions, you realize that whatever is triggering you is simply an experience in which you encounter a feeling around a particular circumstance or situation that is based on some conditioned meaning that you are automatically creating from a past experience . . . and you can pull the plug on the power source!

Living by the 5 EMP Questions will give you a clear understanding of why you go into emotional states (let your Kid grab the wheel), allow you to take actions from these emotional states, and thus create outcomes that aren't what you intended. These questions will become a compass to continually discovering remnants of your outdated conditioning and expired programming. You'll begin to anticipate and neutralize these triggers before they even happen.

## WHAT TO CREATE AND WHERE TO GO FROM HERE?

> *Each of us is an artist of our days; the greater*
> *our integrity and awareness, the more original*
> *and creative our time will become.*

—JOHN O'DONOHUE, *TO BLESS THE SPACE*
*BETWEEN US: A BOOK OF BLESSINGS*

You sensed that there was more opportunity to be found in the life you were living, regardless of the results you were manifesting. Operating from your Kid self was never a long-term option for you. It never felt right, did it? You want to achieve big things, win the game, not just meet expectations but shatter them. You knew you couldn't win the long game with external solutions, and you now know that Kid-driven strategies aren't the answer (they're unsustainable and exhausting).

So now it's time to decide. What do you want to create? Decide what that is without worry as to how you're going to get there. Think of how you're going to get there as a small detail that will work itself out later. The universe has countless ways of making things happen that you could never imagine.

To figure out where you're going, you need to look at where you are now. By this point, a typical client and I would have worked together for about two to three months. That's how long I've found that it takes for someone to realize they have been run by their Kid for countless years. Now clients begin to recognize their triggers and the resulting havoc they have caused for themselves. So let's take a look at that in your life. What is your current experience? In what areas are you replicating patterns that have been with you since childhood? What areas of your life have been impacted by the work you've done in this book so far? Where has the fog lifted for you?

## EXERCISE: *Rate the 10 Areas of Your Life*

In this classic exercise, rate your life in each of the ten areas on a scale of 1 to 10 with 1 being unfulfilled and 10 being fulfilled. Thereafter, write what it would take to make each area a 10—for example, if you rated finances 6, what would you need in that area of life to experience it as a 10? Take the opportunity as you're working through this exercise to honestly examine where you're feeling gratitude and abundance and where you feel a lack of it. To help you with your ratings, ask yourself these questions in each of the ten areas:

1. **Family**—Do you feel like you have enough time? Are you creating magic moments? How is your relationship with your siblings, parents, and extended family?

2. **Primary relationship**—Do you feel connected in love? Do you feel seen and heard? Do you feel like you make a worthy partner?

3. **Physical health**—Do you feel vital, strong, and healthy? Are you getting enough exercise? Do you treat your body well? How do you experience your physical appearance when you look in the mirror?

4. **Spiritual well-being**—How's your spiritual practice? Do you have one? What is your relationship with a God of your understanding? Do you feel connected?

5. **Mental/emotional health**—How do you feel on a daily basis? What are you doing to grow and develop yourself? Are you growing emotionally? Are you learning new things?

6. **Social life**—Do you have a supportive community? Do you have time for friends? This is not about frequency but the quality of your social interactions.

7. **Recreation**—What do you do for fun? Do you have fulfilling hobbies? When was the last time you had a great time?

8. **Contributions**—Do you donate time or money to the causes that you believe in? How do you feel that you're making a contribution?

9. **Business**—How's your current job? How are your current prospects? Do you feel fulfilled in your current role? How is your professional life in general?

10. **Financial**—Are you comfortable and content? Do you have a financial plan? Do you feel financially secure?

## Your Ratings

### 1. Family: _____

*What will it take to make this area a 10?*

_____

_____

### 2. Primary relationship: _____

*What will it take to make this area a 10?*

_____

_____

### 3. Physical health: _____

*What will it take to make this area a 10?*

_____

_____

### 4. Spiritual well-being: _____

*What will it take to make this area a 10?*

_____

_____

### 5. Mental/emotional health: _____

*What will it take to make this area a 10?*

_____

_____

**6. Social life:** _____

*What will it take to make this area a 10?*

_____

_____

**7. Recreation:** _____

*What will it take to make this area a 10?*

_____

_____

**8. Contributions:** _____

*What will it take to make this area a 10?*

_____

_____

**9. Business:** _____

*What will it take to make this area a 10?*

_____

_____

**10. Financial:** _____

*What will it take to make this area a 10?*

_____

_____

The truth is that your life experience is just that—an experience —and there's no reason you can't live your life as a 10 across the board.

*People say that what we're all seeking is a meaning for life. I don't think that's what we're really seeking. I think that what we're seeking is an experience of being alive so that our life experiences on the purely physical plane will have resonances within our own innermost being and reality so that we actually feel the rapture of being alive.*

—JOSEPH CAMPBELL, *THE POWER OF MYTH*

## EXERCISE: *Letter to Your Future Self*

Now that you know the areas of life you want to improve, it's time to stretch yourself. What comes next is from a powerful technique called future pacing, a neuro-linguistic programming (NLP) that helps you experience what could be as if it has already happened.

When I first did this in 2005, I wrote down that I wanted to make a difference in the lives of individuals and organizations, I wanted to live a geographically independent life—spending six months of my year near the ocean and six months in the mountains—and to make a healthy six figures working three days a week and living in a home where I could see the sunrise and the sunset every day. But I couldn't imagine the other amazing things that would happen in addition to what I had dreamed up in my letter . . . because at the time I wrote that I had allowed myself to DREAM BIG. Not only did everything I wrote about come true, but I also found myself expanding in other ways that I couldn't have imagined previously. For example, I could have never imagined getting to travel around the world working with international clients from Europe, Afghanistan, India, Vietnam, Russia, Dubai, and Australia.

1. Envision yourself five years in the future: You are living the outcome-driven life that you've been craving. What does that look

like for you? Think about it in as much detail as possible. How can you make those areas of your life that are 6s and 7s into 10s?

2. Date your letter five years in the future and address it to yourself today. Your future self is writing to your current self and telling you how amazing life is.

3. Write about the experience you want to have five years in the future. See it as already happening. Be as concrete as possible. Really see your life as you'd like it to be in as much detail as possible. You are already living the life of your dreams. You are living where you want, doing what you want for a living, with close friends and/or family you adore. Money's not an issue. In fact, nothing is an issue because this is your dream life, your outcome-driven life. You've done it. You've made it. What does that look like? Think of the kind of life that would make you say, "Wow, that's a really great outcome!" Include each of the ten areas of your life. What would the areas of your life look like as you describe them in as much detail as possible?

4. Really revel in the emotion of it all and truly create a connection to the life you are envisioning for yourself. Make it REAL. Have fun with this and Dream BIG!

5. WARNING: Watch how much resistance comes up here. You're working from a space of unlimited potential—a place of creation rather than a place of reaction. When our brains have been in reaction mode for years, it can be challenging to envision new hopes and dreams from scratch. Watch how much your Kid wants to react as you Dream BIG. He will tell you every reason in the world why this letter is stupid, crazy, never-gonna-happen, a waste of your time, and so on. How do you ever expect to do this? You're too dumb, lazy, and a ridiculous dreamer. Again, the Kid is trying to protect you, but by doing so, he can completely undermine the

exercise if you let him. Remind your Kid that you got this, you're happy to drive the bus, and that he can take a break and relax. The King is in control, so he can hand over the keys now. Remind him how many amazing things have occurred for you in the past and how many more are sure to lie ahead.

## THE WORST-CASE SCENARIO

Exploring the worst-case scenario is one of the most effective practices I have seen for helping my clients live out on that edge and confront their fears. Writing the letter from your future self probably put your Kid on objection overload. The next exercise is about addressing all his concerns.

Remember that the Kid is all about emotional survival. Any time we decide to change our lives, such as moving, changing jobs, buying a house, etc., the internal chaos has always been turned up because the Kid doesn't want to get it wrong. The Kid's favorite question is "HOW will I ever be able to do this?" This question is a dream killer, and the net effect is that it can put your adult self in freeze mode. You think, *I'd better not do anything.* You accept doubts and adopt them as being realistic, practical, or sensible. After all, there's no way you're going to accomplish all that you put in the letter if your Kid even let you finish it.

The risk-averse Kid has told you, in every way he can think of, that you don't have time for dreams anymore, that you have responsibilities, and that your focus needs to be on making money, supporting your family, paying your mortgage, etc. In other words, you need to be a grown-up and focus on taking care of all those adult things that will keep you safe. Of course, the Kid knows how to get inside your head and voice these objections in a way that will specifically play on your deepest insecurities . . . because he lives inside your head!

## EXERCISE: *The Worst-Case Scenario Letter*

The antidote to all of this Kid resistance is to confront what your Kid thinks will be the absolute worst-case scenario created by the letter you just wrote.

1. Reread the Letter from Your Future Self. Let your brain go to all the supposedly horrible things that could happen if you were to pursue all that was possible, as presented by your future self.

2. Write a letter to yourself from your Kid's perspective, telling you all the ways things will go wrong. Let your brain go as far as it wants with this. How bad does it get? Could you be living under a bridge in a cardboard box? Does everyone hate you? Do you lose everything? (Writing down your thoughts allows them to stand still and separates them from the brain's ongoing chatter.)

3. Now apply King logic. You will discover—if you haven't already—that you are incredibly intelligent and resourceful. Things will never get as bad as your Kid wants you to believe they will. For example, I realized that my worst-case scenario is that I would be bartending in a spectacular ski area. And, truthfully, that didn't sound all that bad. In actuality, I knew it would never even get that bad because I know myself to be quite resourceful. Taking a look at this scenario through the King's lens was eye-opening and provided me with some much-needed grounding.

4. Debunk the Kid logic by inserting your King self. Take an honest look at your fears around what would happen if you actually lived your fully realized life. You may find that the language you encounter in the resistance may sound familiar: "I could never." If you catch yourself thinking or saying something out of habit, ask yourself, "Is what I'm thinking or saying true?" Respond to the Kid's fear with the King's assurances.

A Worst-Case Scenario Letter can be written anytime you're in transition—for example, when you're trying to make a big decision like moving, changing jobs, buying a house, or starting something new. The Kid doesn't want to get it wrong, so your worst-case scenarios will always bubble to the surface, feeling real and even imminent.

The Worst-Case Scenario Letter helps you see how entrenched you've become in your routines. It also helps you unwind outdated beliefs and see that change doesn't have to be scary. You've literally done things for the *first time* your whole life. Don't let your age, current circumstances, the fact that you've been out of the job market for a couple of years, or your conditioned mind stop you from dreaming big. Remember Tim's story? When you're done writing the worst-case scenario letter, take a moment to write down ten reasons why making that decision would be the best thing in your life! GO FOR IT!

## HAVE A LITTLE FAITH

One of the most powerful experiences I had in life was in my first real job as an interviewer and ghostwriter for my first mentor David Silver's book *Enterprising Women: Lessons from 100 of the Greatest Entrepreneurs of Our Day.* I was a young man when I went to interview a very successful entrepreneur in Texas who had founded an interior design firm. As the interview wound down, I asked her, "So, what's next for you?"

She looked at me from across her grand desk (everything's bigger in Texas, of course) and leaned in a little closer. In her charming Texan drawl, she said, "Shasheen, I just don't have the creativity to answer that question. If you had told me a year ago that I would be on a flight to New York City, sitting in first class with a glass of champagne and speaking to my Japanese neighbor across the aisle—with the one Japanese word I knew, *kon'nichiwa*—and that it would lead to the biggest design deal in the twenty-year history of this firm, I would have said, 'C'mon, what are you talking about?' Or, if you would have told me that I'd be on a safari in Africa and meet the most extraordinary man and that I'd be engaged six months later, I would have said, 'What are you smoking?' But you know what, Shasheen? That's what happened."

Her stories are some of my favorites because she taught me quite a bit. Yes, we have goals we are driving toward. But there's also an elegant simplicity from not always knowing how things will happen—just know that they are, in fact, going to work out. I liked her philosophy on life: If you show up every day, don't cheat anyone, clean up your messes, and act in kindness, the universe has an interesting way of working things out. So while goal setting is essential, don't leave yourself so rigid that you can't imagine additional possibilities too. Here's a practice that can capture the miracles and magic that have happened in your own life.

## EXERCISE: *Miracle Board*

Many years later when the Law of Attraction and vision boards started to gain popularity, I couldn't forget the lesson that the founder of the interior design firm had taught me. I made a few vision boards and it never really resonated. My mentor at the time, Matthew, told me he liked doing Miracle Boards better.

Miracle Boards are simply a way of acknowledging and documenting what he called the "unexpected good fortune." By declaring the unexpected as miracles and noticing them every day, the brain starts to look for the unexpected good in the world. The idea is similar to a vision board, but instead of its purpose being to envision things you want, the Miracle Board serves to remind you what amazing things continue to occur in spite of ourselves.

What kills our dreams and/or the possibilities ahead is the Kid's desire for certainty, security, and the need for understanding the how's. The Miracle Board allows you to remind your Kid how many serendipitous things have already happened to you. (Practicing meditation and gratitude are just two of the ways through which unexpected good fortune will seem to show up even more for you.)

Take some time to reflect on the serendipitous, good things, the miracles that have occurred in your life. Write them down. Put them up on a board, include photos or mementos that help you remember these events clearly.

Every year, when I review the goals that I've achieved, I also take time to acknowledge and declare all the unexpected good fortune that occurred the prior year—all the things I didn't create on my own or plan out or set goals for.

## WELCOME TO THE EDGE

I urge you to start imagining again. Reimagine your life. Reimagine the new relationship with yourself that will allow you to move with ease and grace through anything life throws your way. Start getting excited about the future.

What is one action you could take today that would move you closer to doing something you've been dreaming about? Instead of coming up with reasons why it won't work, ask yourself, "How can I make this work?" Begin looking into all the possibilities with an open heart and mind.

The invitation I extend to you is one that will take you to the very edge of your comfort zone. And once you're there, I want you to take a long look around. You now know what the Kid is telling you and why. You know that your success strategies have expired and that it's time for a new plan. It's time to create. It's time for something more.

Don't be bound by the experiences of the past as presented by your Kid. You do not have to be bound by past conditioning and a belief system that was put on you rather than created by you. Create new strategies. Explore what's available to you on the edge of possibility.

*There are two basic motivating forces: fear and love. When we are afraid, we pull back from life. When we are in love, we open to all that life has to offer with passion, excitement, and acceptance. We need to learn to love ourselves first, in all our glory and our imperfections. If we cannot love ourselves, we cannot fully open to our ability to love others or our potential to create. Evolution and all hopes for a better world rest in the fearlessness and open-hearted vision of people who embrace life.*

—JOHN LENNON

CONCLUSION

# The Greatest Gift

"He just doesn't get it!" I exclaimed as I hung up the phone. I was 3,000 miles away, and he could still push my buttons.

My dad and I had come so far over the years, but I still got triggered when we spoke. I was forty but was reacting as my ten-year-old self. I went from hating the man and being continuously angry as a teenager to agreeing to disagree about certain subjects as an adult. I felt that our relationship was improving. I would have told you even as a triggered forty-something that I loved my father and that we had a good relationship, and that would have been truthful.

My dad and I never gave up trying to have the father-son relationship we wanted and that both of us believed was possible. However, we had never fully tapped into our true relationship potential either. I often found myself feeling self-righteous and disappointed whenever we spent time together.

After this particular phone call making Christmas plans, I finally had a moment of clarity. I realized I could either continue the dark thoughts in my head around this relationship or start asking the right questions—not of him but of myself. I needed to look inward, not outward. He was being my mirror, not my judge and jury. Why was I getting triggered when we spoke? What was it I really wanted that I wasn't getting from our interactions?

I let both of my personas—my Kid and my King—speak up as I listened to the answers to this question. I wanted my father's appreciation. I wanted him to be interested in me and my life. I wanted him to be proud of me. I wanted him to be more communicative. I wanted him to be fun. I wanted him to be less judgmental and less critical.

Of course, the reality is that age has no bearing on the fact that we will always be our parents' child, whether we're five, fifteen, or forty-five. On some level, we will always want our mommy or daddy. Parenting doesn't have a finish line, and neither does being someone's child. Despite my age at the time, I still wanted to be good enough and lovable enough to have my dad's attention. At that moment, I finally understood the power of a prayer that had been hanging on my wall for several years:

> *Lord make me an instrument of your peace*
> *Where there is hatred, let me sow love*
> *Where there is injury, pardon*
> *Where there is doubt, faith*
> *Where there is despair, hope*
> *Where there is darkness, light*
> *And where there is sadness, joy*
> *O divine master grant that I may*
> *not so much seek to be consoled as to console*
> *To be understood as to understand*
> *To be loved as to love*
> *For it is in giving that we receive*
> *It is in pardoning that we are pardoned*
> *And it is in dying that we are*
> *born to eternal life.*
>
> —SAINT FRANCIS OF ASSISI

Although I consider myself to be more spiritual than religious, the idea of "in giving that we receive" resonated. I inventoried my part in our relationship. In truth, I had been giving my father next to nothing. It was a zero-sum game where I was viewing his gain as my loss and his loss as my gain. I had been withholding love, a pattern I realized was also showing up in my personal relationships.

I never appreciated or acknowledged how amazing he was—his journey from his childhood in India to the abundance he had created in the United States. I never gave him (or my mom) credit for how hard they had worked for every dollar they earned or the sacrifices they made for my sister and me, not to mention for their own brothers and sisters. I never acknowledged what a dreamer and visionary my father had been to put himself through medical school with limited resources. To marry my mom, board a ship to America, and land on the west side of Manhattan with two bags and ten dollars.

I never appreciated how hard his own father pushed him or how much pressure he must have experienced as the eldest of nine siblings. I never appreciated that he grew up under the rule of the fist and yet never laid a hand on my sister or me. I never showed any interest in his life. I had no idea what his days were like, what he was doing in his retirement, or his plan for the next phase of his life. I had never expressed any pride in being his son or pride in our family. On the rare instances that I did talk to him, I would hardly speak, let alone ask him questions or respond with anything but brevity.

At the ripe age of forty, I was still holding on to the narrative that he would take anything I said and turn it against me. My Kid was running rampant all over this relationship, and I was letting him. I was on the offensive, and my Kid was most definitely driving this bus. I would find myself commenting on everything I could find wrong, out of place, old, dirty—whatever I could use to point out that he too had flaws. (My Kid was trying to prove that he wasn't the only one who messed up, wasn't perfect, or sometimes got 99 percent!)

I felt nauseated as I came to this realization. Holding on to this residual childhood resentment and anger was impacting everything in my life. It showed up in my personal relationships in the form of oversensitivity. It showed up in my work life with my disregard for rules and authority. It showed up as cynicism, as weary resignation about the state of the world, and as negative opinions in numerous other areas. So, I took a page from the Prayer of Saint Francis, and I turned it into a question: *Who do I need to be to give to my dad everything I have been asking of him?*

Now, the first time I said that out loud, my immediate reaction was "Hell no! No way. He owes me." I doubled down on my intention to change our relationship despite my initial indignation. I decided to flip the script by beginning to ask him simple questions like "What are your plans today?" I came to know a remarkable man who I would have never known otherwise.

I got to really be with him and learn about his world. I remember his excitement when he responded to my genuine curiosity and interest in his life for the first time. He lit up like the Christmas tree in our living room, and I can remember seeing the joy on his face as the Kid inside him began to get what he had always needed. I realized that this was the first time I gave my father the chance to really be seen and heard.

The entire holiday week had been about the decision to go home and make an effort to do things differently, to seek not to be understood but to be understanding. Because of that decision, aside from his being an esteemed vascular surgeon, I learned that my dad had recently achieved emeritus status as a faculty member at the New York Medical College and was focusing his time with my mom on philanthropic activities. Also, he volunteered his time teaching math to adults who were going for their GEDs and was traveling back and forth to India to support children's education. He had even been helping older people with varicose vein treatments. He actually loved being the senior who got to walk the halls of his new office with younger people. I loved hearing about his experiences and seeing his excitement.

When I looked at all the things I'd been complaining about—that my dad wasn't curious, sincere, or communicative with me—I realized I wasn't there for him. He was actually all those things when I took the time to be those things myself.

I went back to visit my dad at Christmas with a sincere and earnest desire to be the person I wanted him to be. The moment I allowed my outcome-driven King to be in control of the situation, my life quite literally changed overnight.

As we sat down to Christmas dinner, I asked my dad if we had any family traditions about gratitude or giving thanks. My dad replied, "You're the coach, go ahead."

I honored my father by giving him a heartfelt acknowledgment for who he is, what he had accomplished, and what he had created for our family. And, most important, I honored him for his part in who I turned out to be. When I was done speaking, the Christmas present, the one I had given up on long ago while lying on some therapist's couch, appeared.

When it came to his turn to express gratitude, there was not a dry eye at the table as my dad said, "Shasheen, my son, I'm proud of the man that you are today."

Everyone there had known the tumultuous relationship that he and I had shared over the years. And from that moment forward, life has never been the same for me or the rest of our family.

## THE SURPRISING SECRET

The greatest gift this book can give you is not wealth and higher performance and material possessions (though it can give you those and more). No. The greatest gift is enriched relationships with those closest to you: spouses and partners and children and parents and team members. When my high-achieving clients first came to me, they were frustrated with issues like taking their business and results to the next level, getting team members to perform better, making the transition from individual achiever to great leader, and living a more fulfilled life.

But . . . often, beneath the surface, they were also struggling with strained personal relationships and a lack of connection. The surprise gift my clients received (and infinitely more valuable) is repaired and revived relationships with others.

How can you have a reengaged and reignited life and have poor relationships with the people closest to you? The secret to these better relationships is the same secret that ended their inner struggle: compassion. You see, when you begin to have compassion for yourself, it ends the inner struggle with your Kid. It opens the door to a new relationship with yourself. And, in the same way, it opens the door to better relationships with others. In fact, many of my clients are surprised when they find the relationships with others improving as a natural consequence of improving the relationship with themselves— with their Kid.

While not apparent at first, it only makes sense: The harder you are on yourself, the harder you are on others. The harder you are on others, the more miserable you are as a human being. Operating from a place of nonjudgment, love, and compassion for yourself will get you much closer to the life you want to lead than a slash and burn battle plan ever could. As a result of this new approach, strained relationships with spouses and partners and kids and parents begin to heal. They become richer, deeper, and more connected.

Their leadership of their companies and teams improves dramatically. And as it does, their performance and profits also improve. And not because they started working harder and using more force—but because they learned to have compassion for themselves. And that compassion expanded to impact others.

*Love and compassion are necessities, not luxuries.*
*Without them humanity cannot survive.*
—DALAI LAMA

## THE JOURNEY

In this book's opening chapters, you first learned to understand how the Kid has been conditioned to react by both biology and your early life. You gained insight into why you suffer this inner struggle as a high achiever. Then that understanding leads to compassion. You are human, and all humans have these reactivity patterns. So, you quit shaming yourself and have some sympathy for the human you are.

Compassion unlocks the door to ending the war within yourself. Instead of fighting ever harder, you can release the struggle. As the inner struggle subsides and inner calm and stillness enter, you gain incredible clarity into your reactions and, ultimately, into the outcomes you desire. From this understanding and compassion and clarity, you can use the Emotional Mastery Process to eliminate external triggers that rob you of a fulfilled, deeply satisfying life. And as you gain emotional mastery, you are now able to step into a larger outcome-driven life—the life you were born to live.

Remember: This book is not about the sprint; it's about being successful for the long haul. It's about creating lasting change. This is your new instruction manual, and now it's up to you to take all you've learned and apply it to your life. Decide from here on out what you want to achieve. Don't worry about the how; the universe has a way of materializing outcomes beyond your wildest dreams.

You are now free to move about the universal cabin with your seatbelt light perpetually off. You are now free to go out there and be amazing.

The treasures are within.

Your King holds the key.

Compassion is the door.

*— (This is just) the Beginning —*

# Acknowledgments

Gabriela, my one and only Pontouf. Thanks for letting me in and allowing me to find my Crown. The greatest gift has been bearing witness to your extraordinary journey. I am in awe and so proud of the woman you have become.

My Sister Soni, thank you for always having my back, being my sanity check and enduring so many of the challenging moments and rants of my life's journey. I love and appreciate you.

Caleb Silver, thank you for the continued friendship and support for the past 30+ years and always making the time to engage. This finished product could not have happened without your keen meticulous eye, editorial perspective, and advocacy.

Lindsay Andreotti, for enthusiastically and lovingly holding my hand in the beginning of this book's journey and for never letting go.

Matthew Ferry, for taking a chance on this wild card and opening me up to an entire new world of possibilities.

John Assaraf, for your continued friendship, advocacy, inspiration, and our game-changing chairlift rides.

Kim Weiss and The Book Couple (Carol and Gary Rosenberg), for helping me get this book to the finish line!

Robert Stover, who as an advocate of the reader and content of this book, brilliantly structured, translated, and distilled the original manuscript into an easy-to-read and impactful final product.

Bear, for rescuing me and reminding me every day what it looks like to be engaged and lit up by the world.

And last, but not least, Mom and Dad.

This book could not exist without the influences of:

The Wolverton School of Mastery, CRI Worldwide, John Assaraf, Eckhart Tolle, Gary Zukav, Jiddhu Krishnamurti, Werner Erhard, Landmark Worldwide, The Hoffman Institute, Byron Katie, Brene Brown, David Deida, Gay Hendricks, Ram Dass, David and Jerri Silver, Caleb and Analuz Silver, Claude Silver, , Matthew Ferry, Steven Sadlier, Shama Viola, Jasmuheen, Rasha, Swami Bhramdev, Althea Gray, Tony Robbins, Lisa Sasevich, Eric Berne, David McNally, Barry Terry, Bill Wilson, Naomi Fiske, Jacques D'Amboise, The National Dance Institute. Susan Lapointe, Gabriela Rivera, Randy Dobson, Nguyen Xuan Lan, Huyen Phan Dieu, John Margerison, Bob and Estrella Posey & Discovery Programs, Jay Grab, Jane Jones, Adriana Ochoa Margarain, Lynn Wilson, Steven Love, Drew Horning, Lynn and Randall G-Scott, Andrea Minkow, Mark VonMusser, Brook Bishop, Ben Austin, Jayne Jewell, Brenda Schinke, Elaine Holland, Melissa Purdue, Jessie Torres, Matthew Haddad, Sommers Randolph, Frank and Mary Yates, Ron Proulx, Moira Nordholdt, Debra Malmazada, Geraldine Green, Elliot Rappaport, Raj Lahoiti, Andy Serwin, Chris Meyers, Joe Dalessandro, Pam Saunders. Team Peloton: Robin Arzon, Matt Wilpers, Christine D'Ercole, Lianne Hainsby, Dennis Morton, Ally Love, Emma Lovewell, Kendall Toole, Alex Toussant and the #Pelovegans. Brianna Greenspan, Josh Eidenberg, Julie Reisler, Lisa Reuff, Bobby Kountz, Michael O'Brien, Gerald Parr, Margarita Coale, Michael Keogh, Kerri Zaldastani, Maura

# ACKNOWLEDGMENTS

Malini Hoffman, Todd Tononi, Jay Einbender, Kathy Walsh, Alexandra Eldridge, Nigel and Kate Cooper, Lane Segestrom, Alan Epstein, Megan McGowan, Anne Manhart, Alyssa Merwin, Liisa Bozinovic, Kelly Owen, Julie Silverstone, Brianne von Fabrice, Audrey, Kristin & Eli Goodman, Ted and Ami Razatos, Bo Rosser, Kristen Krell, Nicole Curtis, Susan Curtis, Gwendolyn Hubner, Kimberley and Richard Burke, Chuck, Parisa & the Horning Family, Telluride Ski and Golf Club, Erick Goralski, Joelle-Hadley and Ken Alexander, Beth McLaughlin, Shari and Pete Mitchell, Leigh Reneirson, Rosie Cusak, Lorrie Denesik, Penelope Gleason, Kevin O'Connor, Tom and Lucy Maher, Jeff Hauser, Kate Jones, Stewart Seeilegson, Morgan Ballou, Oulli Durham, Robert Stenhammer, DJ Poland, Rachael Shaw Bowers, Bill Goldberg, Don Berman, Rick Greubel, Mark Flitter, Mariza Brimhall, James Maserio, David Salazar, James Campbell Caruso, Sue Oliva, Ramon D'Azua, Shauna Walters, Erica Garcia, Jen Sassen, Brad Hill, Kit Baum, Gerardo Rivera, Mauro Rivera, Thomas Arrey, The Mud Ponies, Heidi Helm and Chris McLarry, Bob Bunten, Jonathan Schaffer, Ezana Gereme, Starfinder Stanley, Eric Gelfand, Robert Murray, Julie Meadow, Julie Kaye, Michael Jamin, The DARLE'S, Starfinder Stanley, EJ Einhorn, Steve Leaden, Carolan Morino, Louis Psihoyos, Lucy Sheils, Carol and Hank Hintemeister, Emily Sacks, Lacy Carlson, Lance Cromwell, Corinne Lebrune, Carrie Fitzgerald, Kim Burt, Sam McDermott, Michelle Barton, Rod McDermott, Jonathan Khorsandi, Andrea Abegglen, Marla Meridith, Jessica Sullivan, Jessica Galbo, Holly Ridgway, Kat V, John Sodano, Jeff Tarr, Crystal Brakhage, Joshua Young, Lance Cromwell, Linda Robinson, Max Strang, Rob Tripplet, Archie Holton, Tomas Thundyil, Paul Middleton, Nick and Ellen Besobrosov The Grumpy Lords and NORDS of Wolverton: Tony Forrest, John Briner, Scott Loss, Dickie Byrne, Jonathan Greenspan, Ed McCashion, Deb Allen, Betsey Adler, Dan Houlihan, Paul Warner, Hawkeye Johnson, Debbie Madaris Craig Stein, Pam Seabolt, Craig Panarisi, Ross Matlock, Jim

Shaw Karen Reader, Scotty McGee, George, Gordon and BJ Briner. Helen Lewis, Stuart Robinson, Terry Williamson, William Carroll, Olga Oslon, Chris Sullivan, Ben & Amanda Ghosh, James Masserio, Mari Tautimes, Leslie Cohen, Courtney Marchesani, Susie Abromeit, Michelle Calo, Farahana Jobanputra, Dane Forte, Ryan Hubris. Colgate Lakehouse Crew: David Ganz, Marshall Bergmann, Chris StPierre, Jon Glickstein, Hy Schwartz, Patrick Shaw, Dan King. The Distinguished members and colorful guests of 52 Broad Street, Colgate University, Julie Silverstone, The Dawn Patrol Board Members, Chad Arendsen, Steve Becker, Victor Curro. NoSiesta Francis Kelsey. The Rustler Lodge, Kate and Tom Pollard, Tauni Powers, Juile and Max Gregoric, Meg Kemp, John Frawley, Ed McCall, Jason Weber, Bradley Prior, Stephen Collins, Chris Bello. Santa Fe Ski Area, Bill Gould, Katya Franzgen, Stew Johnson, Channing, Kevin St John, Steve and Kathy Miller, Chrissy Mahar Miller, Lucy, Waldo, Dan Piburn. Whalen Brady, Tony Masters, Mike Burgoyne, Pat Hall, Justin Anderson, Demian Anderson. Harry, Payton, Kathleen, and Bucky. Aaron Lymer, Jim Bunch, Randy Zales, Dustin Dubois, Alix Bjorklund, Jay Grab. Stephen Cooper, JT McCormick, Jessica Burdg, Erin Carenzo, Jessica Robbins, Linda Love, Margaret Mcbride, Hedi Krupp, Gideon Weil, Joanne McCall, Kelly Notaras. The Entire Shah Family: Morajee Deraj & Jiviben Shah, Pravin & Deena Shah, Sonal & Greg Parr, Rasik, Jyotsna, Anish Shah, Sylvia Rozwadowska, Atul Shah, Tilak, Aruna, Rubin, Riti, Nikin & Rashmi Shah. Ashwin, Monica, Yash, Anokhee Shah. Sudhir, Nirav, & Nikhil Shah. Pushpa, Sanjeev & Elizabeth Shah, Steve & Shilpa Harhart. Jayu, Jayant, Neil & Tina Shah Jason Vogel, Hemant & Madhuri, Pooja, Nimesh Gala,. Mahendra, Heena, Samir and Rahul Shah Kasturi, Nahendra, Shaleen, Vira. Angie, Deepak, Moneesh, Amiti & Mona Bhow. Jay and Jayshree, Amal Shah. Bhupendra and Urmilaben Shah. Jitendra, Divyaben, Padmaben Shah. Photo Credit: Dr Wade Brackenbury.

# References

Berne, MD, Eric. *Games People Play: The Basic Handbook of Transactional Analysis*. New York: Ballantine Books, 1964.

Campbell, Joseph, with Bill Moyers. *The Power of Myth*. New York: Anchor Books, 1988.

Cherry, Kendra. "Erik Erikson's Stages of Psychosocial Development." VeryWell Mind. Updated June 26, 2020. Accessed February 1, 2021. www .verywellmind.com/erik-eriksons-stages-of-psychosocial-development -2795740.

Corey, Gerald. "Transactional Analysis." Acadia University Web Tutor. Accessed February 1, 2021. www.acadiau.ca/~rlehr/Transactional%20 Analysis%20ch%20Corey%202013.

Dispenza, D. C., Joe. *Evolve Your Brain: The Science of Changing Your Mind*. Deerfield Beach, FL: Health Communications, Inc., 2007.

Dostoevsky, Fyodor. *Notes from Underground*. New York: Vintage Books, 1993.

Gladwell, Malcolm. *Blink: The Power of Thinking Without Thinking*. New York: Little, Brown and Co., 2005.

Hendricks, Gay. *The Big Leap: Conquer Your Hidden Fear and Take Life to the Next Level*. New York: HarperCollins, 2009.

Katie, Byron. *Loving What Is: Four Questions That Can Change Your Life*. New York: Harmony Books, 2002.

Krishnamurti, Jiddu. *Freedom from the Known*. New York: HarperCollins Publishers, 1969.

Krishnamurti, Jiddu. *Think on These Things*. New York: Harper & Row Publishers, 1964.

Lipton, Bruce. "How Do We Become Good Parents?" Website of Bruce H. Lipton, PhD. September 1, 2015. Accessed February 1, 2021. www .brucelipton.com/how-do-we-become-good-parents/.

O'Donohue, John. *To Bless the Space Between Us: A Book of Blessings*. New York: Doubleday, 2008.

# About the Author

*"What I encounter again and again is how high achievers—like everyone else—feel deeply estranged, alone and misunderstood in their relationships both business and personal. It is within this hidden struggle that the real transformational work takes place."*
—Shasheen Shah

**Shasheen Shah** is the CEO of Coherent Strategies Consulting and Coaching. For more than 20 years, he has delivered breakthrough results to successful leaders around the world, navigating business outcomes and the personal challenges that go hand in hand with the journey. High-achieving professionals from Tesla, LinkedIn, Hewlett-Packard, IBM, and Ashley Homestores are but a few who have benefited from Shasheen's life-altering coaching skills. In 2012, Tony Robbins hired Shasheen to be one of his exclusive certified Platinum Partner and Business Results Coaches.

Shasheen's life-altering coaching skills and his razor-sharp intuition, combined with his unique ability to tactfully navigate and address life's most confronting conversations, separates him from the rest, allowing him to cut through the barriers that stand in the way of the people with whom he works.

As a philosophy major from Colgate University, Shasheen remains a student and continues to feed his insatiable appetite for understanding the human experience every day, incorporating, integrating, and applying new insights and awareness into breakthrough results for himself as a way of life. Understanding the work and world of Shasheen is to understand who he is from the inside out. Readers, clients, and friends will benefit from the values that serve as his "operating system." They include:

+ Living in and contributing to a kind and compassionate world.

+ Cultivating the art of listening.

+ Teaching people to stop trying to fix what isn't broken.

+ Learning and practicing acceptance.

+ Mentoring young people, entrepreneurs, and our next generation of leaders.

+ Sharing the lifelong commitment to our inner life as a practice not just a quick-fix, shortsighted theory.

+ Serving the greater good (not just ourselves).

+ Embracing and connecting with Mother Nature.

+ Living the life we imagine—starting now!

A native New Yorker with roots in India, Shasheen currently spends his time in Santa Fe, New Mexico, and Telluride, Colorado. Visit him at www.shasheen.com.

Made in the USA
Columbia, SC
12 October 2021

46693155R00113